*Our
Hebrew-Christian
Heritage*

OUR
HEBREW-CHRISTIAN
HERITAGE

By

John P. Milton

STRAUS PRINTING & PUBLISHING CO.
Madison, Wisconsin

Other books by John P. Milton:

Psalms

Prophecy Interpreted

Preaching from Isaiah

Holy Garments

People are Asking

More People are Asking

God's Word to Men

The Way

God's Covenant of Blessing

First Edition
Library of Congress Card Number 73-85714

Copyrighted, 1973 with all rights reserved by
ADULT CHRISTIAN EDUCATION FOUNDATION
Madison, Wisconsin
Printed in United States of America by
STRAUS PRINTING AND PUBLISHING COMPANY
Madison, Wisconsin.

FOREWORD

Any discussion of such a theme as this should stimulate curiosity as to what it means and concern as to its continuing relevance today. To satisfy the curiosity as to what it means should be relatively easy. It may be more difficult to convince ourselves and others to what extent it is still meaningful in the twentieth century A.D. Nevertheless we shall try to do both.

Let us begin with a brief explanation of the theme itself, "Our Hebrew-Christian Heritage." By the use of the pronoun "our" we refer specifically to the Christian Church. It is true that in a secondary sense we might refer to Western culture and civilization since the time of Constantine, in which we can trace a strong influence of the Judaeo-Christian tradition until fairly recent times. To avoid too great diffusion, however, we shall limit ourselves to the Christian Church, where the concept of heritage most fittingly belongs. The word "heritage" suggests something that has been handed down, from Abraham and Moses and the prophets, and from Jesus Christ and the apostles, and from the centuries of the Christian Church, *to us* who live today, and who must now either receive it or reject it; and if we receive it in faith *we pass it on* to generations yet to come, and if we reject it in unbelief we thereby stop it from going further. Faith or unbelief will determine whether it will continue to be "a heritage." The hyphenated word "Hebrew-Christian" may surprise you at first. Why this wording rather than the more common and familiar "Judaeo-Christian tradition?" The answer is quite simple.. We are anxious to avoid any possible suggestion of an equation between "Judaism" and "Christianity," as if there were no essential difference between the two; and at the same time we are anxious to show that in spite of their differences they have much in common, because they both go back to the same Hebrew or Old Testament roots. We are interested in this line of heritage from Abraham to Christ in which two great religions share; but beginning with Jesus Christ we are concerned with the differences which have perpetuated themselves in Judaism and Christianity, so that our "Hebrew-Christian" heritage becomes for us *a Christian heritage*.

As we ask what this Hebrew-Christian heritage is we shall think in terms of *affirmations* or *teachings* or *truths* or *articles of faith* which

5

were held to be *realities,* and therefore shaping both religion and culture, both faith and life. We shall speak also in terms of *concepts,* for it is a convenient word to use; but keep in mind that our Hebrew-Christian heritage is not an intellectual system, such as Greek philosophy: it is not composed of a mere collection of mental ideas, but is rather a dynamic confession of a living religious faith which entered deeply into the experience of God's people. We shall soon see the distinction as we study a few of these "concepts."

One more thing to be kept in mind is that there will necessarily be considerable overlapping as we consider different themes. The reason is obvious: no biblical teaching is completely isolated from any other teaching. They are related one to another as belonging to a unified experience of faith and life. For example, how could one possibly separate between such themes as God, Creation and Man? It is precisely these themes which constitute the fundamentals of our Hebrew-Christian heritage, and it is with them that we shall begin our study; but for the sake of clarity we shall separate them and devote a chapter to each, with subsequent chapters linking up with these three.

One thing more by way of introduction: let me make it quite clear that this book is not written primarily *for the learned,* whether he be theologian, philosopher, or scientist, but *for the humble Christian* and faithful Bible reader who is not quite sure of the full glory and extent of his heritage. If it has any single purpose it is to bring to the reader an experience a little like that which comes with the opening of a will and discovering that we are heirs to much more than we had dared to hope or believe. We have indeed a great and glorious Hebrew-Christian heritage, of which we may rightly use the words of Paul concerning one portion of it, "Thanks be to God for his inexpressible gift!" (II Cor. 9: 15)

TABLE OF CONTENTS

Chapter 1

THE HEBREW-CHRISTIAN CONCEPT OF GOD

What is unique about the Hebrew-Christian affirmation concerning God? Since the Bible is completely theocentric in character we must try to *select* that which is most significant; and no one who has read the Bible with an open mind can escape the significance of the statement that he is *the living God.*

The Living God

The biblical use of the term is divided almost equally between the Old Testament and the New. We cannot look at them all; but six illustrations may serve to represent them all.

One is found in Deut. 5: 26, as a part of the people's reaction to the theophany on Mt. Sinai: "For who is there of all flesh, that has heard the voice of the living God speaking out of the midst of fire, as we have, and has still lived?" Here it is associated with *fear.* Perhaps we could also call it an overwhelming sense of *awe.*

In Ps. 42: 2 it is associated with *a deep yearning* for his presence in worship:

> "My soul thirsts for God,
>   for the living God.
> When shall I come and behold
>   the face of God?"

A similar passage in Ps. 84: 2 brings in a new association, that of *joy*:

> "My soul longs, yea, faints
>   for the courts of the LORD;
> my heart and flesh sing for joy
>   to the living God."

The prophet Jeremiah in Jer. 10: 10 connects it with *the judgment power of God*:

> "But the LORD is the true God;
>   he is the living God and the everlasting King.
> At his wrath the earth quakes,
>   and the nations cannot endure his indignation."

9

Moving into the New Testament we find Simon Peter using it in his great confession of *faith,* on which Jesus promised to build his Church (Mt. 16: 16) : "You are the Christ, the Son of the living God."

And the adjuration of the Jewish high priest on the night of Jesus' arrest and trial shows that the Jews shared this same faith concerning God, though naturally not concerning Christ (Mt. 26: 63) : "I adjure you by the living God, tell us if you are the Christ, the Son of God." Jesus' reply was a simple acknowledgment of *the truth* of the challenge: he was indeed the Son of the living God.

But what is the significance of such an affirmation, of this concept of the living God, which obviously extends far beyond the mere use of the words? At the very minimum it connotes *three* great and glorious things about God. God is! God acts! God speaks!

God is! The Bible does not begin by trying to prove his existence: it shows God in action. This should be evident to even the most casual reader; but it needs to be underscored today, for it is a precious part of our heritage which is in danger of being lost. In one of his earliest books, *The Challenge of Israel's Faith* (1944), G. Ernest Wright has correctly said: "The proposition which is the great gift of Israel to humanity is simply this: *God is.* His existence for the Israelite writer is completely self-evident, always presupposed, and never placed in question." This unquestioning faith is a part of our Hebrew-Christian heritage. Edmond Jacob, in his *Theology of the Old Testament,* calls the affirmation of the sovereignty of God the "force and unity" of the Old Testament and adds, "Moreover, the existence of God is never questioned; only fools can say, 'There is no God' (Ps. 14: 1)." H.H. Rowley gives still another slant to this same truth when he says in *The Faith of Israel,* "The thought of the Old Testament is centered in God. Yet there is nowhere any effort to prove that God exists. For the God of the Old Testament is *the God of experience* and not of speculation." Whether we speak of the Old or of the New Testament *"life* is what differentiates Yahweh from other gods" (Ed. Jacob). This conviction is at the heart of our Hebrew-Christian heritage. He is a living Person, not an impersonal Force. He is capable of action and also of communication. There exists not only the possibility but the reality of a relationship with us which we shall later call the Covenant. For the moment this may suffice, that no one who takes his Hebrew-Christian heritage seriously will ever be tempted to say that God is dead! The Christian as well as the Jew knows better. God is!

However, our Hebrew-Christian heritage goes a step further: it also affirms that *God acts*. He would not be the living God if he did not act. Action is a part of *life*. Quoting Edmond Jacob again: "The Israelite felt God as *an active power* before positing him as an eternal principle." This fact of the action of God has come to be recognized by many Christian theologians as equivalent to, or at least essential to, revelation. In his study book, *The Mightly Acts of God*, Robert Marshall has described the nature of *special revelation* in these words: "Such revelation always includes two elements, (1) a special event and (2) a special person or persons to interpret the event. Thus in the Bible God is revealed in the events of history interpreted by those gifted with special insight." *The interpreter* suggests to us such men as Moses and the prophets and Jesus and the apostles, of whom we shall have more to say later. *The acts* suggest such events as creation, the Exodus redemption, the covenant with Israel, the sending of God's Son to be the Savior of the world. Israel's faith was built on the remembrance of events in their history which the prophet Micah, for example, calls "the saving acts of the LORD" (Mic. 6: 5). In the *Book of the Acts of God* by Wright and Fuller *five events* especially are seen as "faith-events, that is, events which helped to form the Israelite confession of faith." These five are the call of Abraham, the Exodus-redemption, the Sinai covenant, the conquest of Canaan, and the Davidic government. The list could easily be enlarged, and for the Christian must naturally be extended to include the life, death, and resurrection of Jesus Christ, and the history of the Christian church down through the ages. It would not be complete, in fact, without saying that the living God *acts still today* in judgment and in redemption. Because he lives he is at work. This is a precious part of our Hebrew-Christian heritage. Jesus sums it up in Jn. 5: 17, "My Father is working still, and I am working." It is *for faith* to see the deed and to recognize the doer: to affirm that *God acts*.

This recognition, however, does not come readily of itself: it requires that God interpret the event through men whom he has raised up, equipped, and sent. We move therefore to the third aspect of *the living God* which is a part of our Hebrew-Christian heritage: *God speaks*. We have referred earlier to Robert Marshall's statement about *revelation* which connects *the event* with *the person* who interprets the event. We shall wait until later to discuss Moses and the Torah, the word of the LORD which came to the prophets, and the gospel as preached by Jesus and Paul. When we say that *God speaks* we do not base the affirmation on a single phrase, such as "the LORD said to Moses," or "the word of the LORD came to me," or "Thus says the LORD," or even on such a startling assertion as Amos

11

makes (Amos 3: 7-8):

> "Surely the LORD God does nothing,
>   without revealing his secret
>   to his servants the prophets.
> The lion has roared;
>   who will not fear?
> The LORD God has spoken;
>   who can but prophesy?"

These are significant, but they are simply parts of a larger whole; and it is at the larger perspective that we must look. That perspective has been well presented by a writer from another generation (and not all ancient writers are outdated) in this way: "whether we take the Hebrew Scriptures as true or not, *it is an incontrovertible fact* that the fundamental idea of the Hebrew religion is that Jehovah is a God who reveals Himself to His creatures; that He has not left the human race to grope their way to the regions of religion or morality as they best can, but that from the beginning He has taken His children by the hand, cared for their welfare, *made known to them His will,* and marked out for them the way to happiness" (McCaul, *Aids to Faith,* as quoted in Girdlestone's *Synonyms of the Old Testament*). It is of the essence of our Hebrew-Christian heritage that *God speaks* to his people and makes known to them his will. Whether we believe it or not is one thing. It is *an incontrovertible fact* that the men who wrote the Scriptures so believed. It was an essential part of their concept of and experience with *the living God* who is, who acts, and who speaks his interpretive word. This is *our* heritage as well which has come down to us through the centuries.

The Only God

The second affirmation of our Hebrew-Christian heritage concerning God is this that "the LORD our God is *one* LORD" (Deut. 6: 4); or, as the translation in the footnote reads, "the LORD our God, the LORD is *one.*"

This is the truth of monotheism versus polytheism. It is implied already in the first commandment, (Ex. 20: 3), "You shall have no other gods before (or besides) me." The psalmist states it even more clearly, "thou alone art God" (Ps. 86: 10b). We must be careful not to be misled by the frequent references, especially in the Old Testament, to "other gods" who were worshipped by Israel's neighbors but *lacked the reality* of the living God. The New Testament gives the theological explanation of this manner of speech; as when Paul says in I Cor. 8: 5-6, "For although there may be *so-called* gods in heaven or on earth — as indeed there are

12

many gods and many lords — yet for us there is one God, the Father, from whom are all things and for whom we exist, and one Lord Jesus Christ, through whom are all things and through whom we exist." Apart from the Pauline reference to the Lord Jesus Christ, this is also the authentic message of the Old Testament.

But this Oneness of God is never a merely speculative or philosophical assertion in our Hebrew-Christian heritage: it is always a motivation to a similar oneness or wholeheartedness on our part in worship. Because the psalmist says, "thou alone art God," he goes on to say in the next verse, "unite my heart to fear thy name" (Ps. 86: 10, 11). So it is also with the great passage in Deut. 6: 4-9, which the Jews call the Shema: "Hear, O Israel: The LORD our God is one LORD; and you shall love the LORD your God with all your heart, and with all your soul, and with all your might." So important were these words that they were to be written upon the heart as upon a tablet, and they were to be taught and talked about everywhere, in the house and while walking (with some companion) in the way, when going to sleep and when rising again from sleep, and they were to be worn as a sign upon the hands and as frontlets between the eyes, and they were to be written upon the very doors and gates of every Jewish home. They are rated equally high in the New Testament. "This is the great and first commandment," said Jesus to the inquiring lawyer (Mt. 22: 38) and not by accident he placed alongside of it a second, "You shall love your neighbor as yourself" (Mt. 22: 39). Worship of God and service to your neighbor, with all your heart: because God is One, and therefore we are all brothers. Paul catches up the worship refrain in his letter to young Timothy: "To the King of ages, immortal, invisible, the only God, be honor and glory for ever and ever. Amen." (I Tim. 1: 17).

There is therefore a negative and a positive connotation to this Hebrew-Christian concept of *God as One*. On the one hand, it excludes all rivals, it rules out the worship of all other gods, whether conceived of in the form of polytheism (many gods) or of idolatry (images to which deity is ascribed) or a combination of the two. See the first two commandments (Ex. 20: 3-6). On the other hand, it enjoins a similar oneness or wholeness in the worship of God and in the service of one another. It is sadly true that neither the Jewish people nor the Christian church has measured up fully to this ideal; but the fact remains that the ideal has always been there, and is there still today, as the challenge to faith and

13

obedience from our Hebrew-Christian heritage. God is One! We worship his as such in a "person to person" relationship.

What Is God Like?

It might seem futile, if not ridiculous, to attempt to describe God, either as to his nature or his character. As the New Testament clearly states, and the Old Testament, in spite of its many theophanies, implies is he not "spirit" (Jn. 4: 24) and "invisible" (Hebr. 11: 27)? "No one has ever seen God," we read in Jn. 1: 18. "For man shall not see me and live," we read in Ex. 33: 20. Nevertheless our Hebrew-Christian heritage speaks of a God whose essential character can be known by faith on the basis of his acts.

What is God like? There are many ways in which to summarize the biblical doctrine and experience of God. We have already spoken of him as the living God, who is, who acts, and who speaks. Speaking of his characteristics as revealed by his acts H. W. Hertzberg, in *"The Encyclopedia of the Lutheran Church"* (1965), says of him: "The theological statements of the Old Testament about God may be reproduced in *three* short sentences: God is Power, God is Righteousness, God is Grace." All three indicate that God is known through events in which he is seen to act, acts interpreted by men whom he has raised up for that purpose. When I was a child I learned a long Catechism answer to the question, "What is God?" The answer consisted of thirteen assertions about God, most of them in adjective form, and each supported by a Bible verse. There is nothing wrong about that methodology if each assertion, each descriptive adjective, is motivated by an event which faith interprets as an act of God: that is, if it describes the way in which the living God actually revealed himself in relation to his people. G. Ernest Wright does much the same thing in chapter IV of *The Challenge of Israel's Faith*. The theme of the chapter, "For I Am Thy God," is illustrated in part by *four* adjectives which Scripture uses to describe what God is like. God is holy! God is righteous! God is gracious! God is jealous! "The saving acts of God" as recited by the Old Testament history, and as interpreted by Moses and the prophets and the psalmists, and as reaffirmed by the New Testament, are best expressed in terms of adjectives such as these. Each one of them will come in for attention later on; at the moment we select just one of them for closer scrutiny in connection with our study of the living God.

The Holiness of God

The third major affirmation of our Hebrew-Christian heritage concerning God is that he is *holy*.

According to Lev. 19: 2 Moses was to tell the people of Israel, "You shall be holy; for I the LORD your God am holy." The words are echoed in the New Testament, in I Peter 1: 15, 16, "But as he who called you is holy, be holy yourselves in all your conduct; since it is written, 'You shall be holy, for I am holy'." It is, as you will observe, both an affirmation about God and an admonition to us who claim to be the people of God. It also raises a number of questions.

What is meant by the holiness of God?

This quotation may begin to help us see its significance in the biblical religion (our Hebrew-Christian heritage): "By declaring that what was best in the Old Testament could also be found in Greek philosophy, Schleiermacher forgot that *that best* was neither monotheism, nor the immortality of the soul, but the holiness of God." (Ed. Jacob, *Theology of the Old Testament*). If that be true, we must make sure that we understand the meaning of *holiness*.

The meaning of it involves both etymology and usage. If the original or etymological meaning of the Hebrew word was "to be separate," as many believe, then the *holiness* of God is equivalent to his *transcendence*. He is separate in the sense that he is exalted above all creation. He is "the totally other." The word denotes "essential Deity." It says to us that "God is God, and man knows his place before him." The clearest example of this is *the trisagion* in Isaiah 6. In his vision the prophet saw the LORD "sitting upon a throne, high and lifted up," and he heard the continuous antiphonal singing of the seraphim,

> "Holy, holy, holy is the LORD of hosts;
> the whole earth is full of his glory."

The effect was to humble Isaiah in the dust. "Woe is me! For I am lost; for I am a man of unclean lips, and I dwell in the midst of a people of unclean lips; for my eyes have seen the King, the LORD of hosts!" (Is. 6: 5).

But even here we observe that there is more to the biblical concept of holiness than transcendence. There is in actual usage a strong emphasis on *moral purity,* approaching the concept of transcendent righteousness. This is the emphasis of Faber in his hymn, "My God! How Wonderful Thou Art:"

> "How wonderful, how beautiful,
> The sight of Thee must be,
> Thine endless wisdom, boundless pow'r,
> And aweful purity!"

15

Holy is not a synonym for *righteousness*, but neither does it exclude it. God is holy in everything that he is and in all that he does: holy in his faithfulness, holy in his righteousness, holy in his grace and love, holy even in his jealousy which tolerates no rivals. He is holy in his exaltation above men but equally so in his condescension to men. The most beautiful statement of what God's holiness means in our Hebrew-Christian heritage is found in Is. 57: 15,

> "For thus says the high and lofty One
> who inhabits eternity, whose name is Holy:
> 'I dwell in the high and holy place
> and also with him who is of a contrite and humble spirit,
> to revive the spirit of the humble,
> and to revive the heart of the contrite!' "

The complete "otherness" of God does not prevent him from being involved in the affairs of men. It is such a God that our Hebrew-Christian heritage makes known to us! It is such a God that we need. There is no contradiction between his might and his mercy.

> "O God of mercy, God of might,
> In love and pity infinite,
> Teach us, as ever in Thy sight,
> To live our life to Thee!"

It is such a prayer that we are moved to pray when we contemplate the holiness of God. We can never be holy in the same sense of transcendence and moral purity as he; but we can permit ourselves to be *set apart* unto his worship and service, to be dedicated to the pursuit of the same lofty standards of mercy and might as revealed to us by his saving acts: in this sense, if in no other, *we can be holy* as our Hebrew-Christian heritage urges us to be. But it is a verse like Is. 57: 15 that tells us *what the holiness of God* really means for his people. He is the Holy One of Israel both as Ruler and as Redeemer.

THE NAME OF GOD

There is a fourth affirmation concerning God which, though a significant part of the Hebrew-Christian heritage, is often overlooked because it is not understood. We refer to the personal name for the God of Israel, YHWH or the LORD.

The name occurs more than 5000 times in the Old Testament. This is not the place for a lengthy critical discussion of the differing opinions as to the pronunciation, origin, and meaning of the Hebrew word, the so-called *tetragrammaton*, the four consonants of YHWH. A little of its background can be seen by reading the Preface to the Revised Standard Version of the Bible. Wherever in the RSV the English word LORD is spelled with four capital letters it represents the personal Hebrew name YHWH, whose original pronunciation was probably Yahweh. The word Jehovah in the American Standard Version is definitely incorrect. But what concerns us in this study is not the spelling but the probable meaning. Have we any hint in that direction? Personally I think that we do.

In Ex. 3: 13-15, in the story of the theophany of the burning bush and the call of Moses to lead his people out of slavery in Egypt, Moses asks God *by what name* he should make him known to the people of Israel. In reply God gives what seems to be a theological explanation of both the etymology and the meaning of the name YHWH. It may sound like a strangely enigmatic answer: "I AM WHO I AM" (see also the footnote for variant translations). Linguistically it is a translation of the first person singular imperfect of the Hebrew verb *hayah*, which can mean either *to be* or *to become*. It is quite probable that Yahweh is the third person masculine singular imperfect of the same verb. It obviously has something to do with either the concept of *being* or of *becoming*. If the former, the "I AM WHO I AM" might seem to be a claim to *absolute existence*, and a rebuke to Moses as if he were impudent even to ask about it: for is not God essentially the *unknowable* One? But the context does not indicate arebuke so much as an explanation. There is much to support S. R. Driver's excellent definition of *Yahweh* as "Self-manifesting existence." It is as if God says to Moses and Israel: You ask who I am, what is my name? You shall *learn to know* when you *see the acts* that I am about to perform in your behalf. In the offing, of course, was that most significant of all "faith-events" in Israel's history, the Exodus-redemption and the Sinaitic covenant. Of these we shall have more to say in later chapters. Gerhard von Rad seems to agree with Driver's interpretation, though he expresses it somewhat differently (in his little book titled *Moses*). According to von Rad the better translation in Ex. 3: 13-15 is "I will be that which I will be," and its reference (and therefore also of the name YHWH) is to "being in act" rather than to "being at rest." The name asserts God's presence in his condescension to men and in his activity which makes them aware of his willingness to help.

The best biblical summary of this activity is found in Ex. 34: 5-8, a proclamation of the name of the LORD and of its essential meaning. "And the LORD descended in the cloud and stood with him there, and proclaimed the name of the LORD. The LORD passed before him, and proclaimed,

'The LORD, the LORD, a God merciful and gracious, slow to anger, and abounding in steadfast love and faithfulness, keeping steadfast love for thousands, forgiving iniquity and transgression and sin, but who will by no means clear the guilty, visiting the iniquity of the fathers upon the children and the children's children, to the third and fourth generation.' And Moses made haste to bow his head toward the earth, and worshiped." Such is the meaning of the name YHWH, the LORD, which is such a vital part of our Hebrew-Christian heritage: a God who acts continually in salvation but also in judgment. Perhaps we see and recognize his judgments more often, because they are more spectacular when directed against the nations; his salvation is quieter and more personal, but just as powerful and real.

What we have said thus far by no means exhausts what even the Old Testament has given us by way of a heritage concerning the living God. The concept of God will be seen in every succeeding chapter; for the Bible, as we have already said, is theocentric from beginning to end. We look forward especially to what the New Testament has to say about God who is One and yet also Triune. We conclude *this introduction* to the Hebrew-Christian concept of God with a few additional suggested Bible readings:

Ps. 145 God is *great,* and God is *good*: his greatness is unsearchable, and his goodness is abundant.

Ps. 139 The Omniscient and Omnipresent Omnipotence of God (Franz Delitzsch).

Is. 40 The soaring ode to God's sovereignty, in creation and in history.

Ezek. 1 "The appearance of the likeness of the glory of the LORD," imagistically described.

Pss. 6 and 130 Note especially Ps. 86: 5, where W.O.E. Oesterley translates "forgive" instead of "forgiving." God is a *forgiver*. It belongs to his very nature to forgive sins. This is also the testimony of Ps. 130: 4, "But there is forgiveness with thee, that thou mayest be feared."

The same emphasis is found in countless places in the Old Testament, especially in the Psalms.

Ps. 23 The LORD is my shepherd, who provides, protects, and grants unending goodness and mercy, here on earth, and in heaven forever.

Ps. 27 The LORD is my light and my salvation and the strength of my life, who banishes all fears.

We could continue. It is not necessary for our purpose to do so. The point that we have tried to make is that if we take our Hebrew-Christian heritage seriously, we have a wonderful God! And no one has succeeded yet in getting rid of him! He is the One true and only living God, with whom we may have a living fellowship if we choose.

Chapter 2

THE HEBREW-CHRISTIAN CONCEPT OF CREATION

We have said that one of the chief characteristics of the Hebrew-Christian concept of *the living God* is that he is *a God who acts.*

We encounter this activity in the very first sentence of Genesis. God is the Creator. The universe, and all that exists, is created. We therefore rightly speak of a Creator-creation relationship. There is a double aspect to this biblical doctrine of creation, illustrated in this Collect from the *Lutheran Service Book and Hymnal* (1958): "O God, at whose word chaos became an ordered creation: Brood over this troubled world as once thy Spirit moved upon the face of the waters, and create in the nations such love for thee and for each other, that this world may be a new creation in righteousness, peace and brotherhood: through thy Son, Jesus Christ our Lord. Amen." Prayer No. 66. (p. 227).

Before we consider this concept of creation let us briefly review our perspective of the biblical concept of God. According to our Hebrew-Christian heritage God is a personal Being, the living God, who is and who acts and who speaks; the One and only God, who is to be whole-heartedly worshipped and served; the Holy God, whose holiness includes both transcendence and aweful purity, and at the same time consummate mercy and compassion: "the totally other," who nevertheless is always near, whose personal name Yahweh denotes "self-manifesting existence" (Driver) or "being in act" (von Rad); so that it can truthfully be said that "in faith of the Old Testament the *Name* of God and *his saving will* are inseparably held together" (von Rad, *Moses,* p. 25).

From here on every theme that we consider will involve some act of God, so interpreted by Moses and the prophets and Jesus and the apostles: for our Hebrew-Christian heritage is completely *God-centered.* Among these acts of God the Bible in its present format gives *priority to creation.* At the beginning of the Old Testament are the two "creation chapters," Genesis 1 and 2; and at the end of the New Testament, in Revelation 21 and 22, we see "a new heaven and a new earth," and we hear the word of him who sits upon the throne, "Behold, I make all things new" (Rev. 21: 5). The Holy Scriptures as they have been given to us begin and end on the note of divine creation; and the concept reoccurs again and again in the intervening chapters, some of which we shall examine later.

The Meaning of Creation

What do we mean when we speak of *Creation?* We think now specifically of our Hebrew-Christian heritage. Before analyzing Genesis 1, the chief biblical confession concerning creation, it may be helpful to look at a few independent interpretations of the concept in general.

Gustaf Wingren of Lund, in a book called *Creation and the Law* (a translation from Swedish), emphasizes *the priority* of the act of creation among the acts of God. He notes that in both the Apostles' and the Nicene Creeds *the first article* speaks of creation, not of redemption, because in the Bible creation comes first. That is, whoever edited the Pentateuch as a confession of faith, and whenever this edition took place with reference to its several parts, *creation was given the place of honor at the beginning.* It stands first among the acts of God which constitute our Hebrew-Christian heritage.

In chapter 4 of *The Bible: Book of Faith* (Augsburg, 1964), the present writer has expanded this question of priority so as to include the question of *origin.* Of the two, priority is the more important theologically. "It is not necessary that we be able to determine exactly how or when this doctrine of creation received the clear formulation given it in Genesis 1. The very fact that it was placed first in the Old Testament canon is significant. — When we ask about the date and origin of Genesis 1, we are concerned about *the manner of the revelation* rather than with *the substance of the message.* In whatever way God by his Word chose to use, Israel was led to the conviction *that creation belonged first among the acts of God."* If the reader is interested in *opinions as to the process* by which this conviction came about he might take time to read a little more in the book and chapter just quoted; but what matters most is the fact of the conviction: that we see Genesis I in its right light as a confession of faith.

Of equal significance is a quotation from Dietrich Bonhoeffer's *Creation and Fall* concerning *the beginning.* After a lengthy quotation which he puts in the mouth of the evil one, a liar from the beginning, he presents this alternative: "Either he is speaking, or the other One who, from the beginning, was the way, the truth, and the life, who was in the beginning: God himself, Christ, the Holy Spirit" (p. 11). Then comes the punch line: "No one can speak of the beginning but the one who was the beginning. Thus the Bible begins with God's free affirmation, free asknowledgment, free revelation of himself: In the beginning God created—." In other words, the origin of this conviction and confession concerning creation, whatever the human process of its formulation, is ultimately *faith based on God's self-revelation.* As such it is a fundamental characteristic of Hebrew-Christian culture.

Helmut Thielicke calls creation "a kind of prophecy turned backwards" (*How the World Began,* p. 18); and he adds that the biblical writers were not primarily interested in "the condition of the world before history began" but rather in "the certainty that here, before the foundation of the world, there begins the history of a great love and a great search." This is *obviously religious language,* both on the part of Bonhoeffer and of Thielicke, and it is very much a part of our Hebrew-Christian heritage. As Thielicke puts it, "So I cannot read the story of creation without seeing that I am in it too;" that is, it concerns my life because it bears witness to the fact that the living God, the Creator, is *with me all the way.*

There is a threefold *theological* interpretation of the biblical doctrine of creation in Edmond Jacob's *Theology of the Old Testament* that shows us a little more of the length and breadth and depth of our Hebrew-Christian heritage. First he says, "For Israel creation marks a commencement." If we ask: a commencement of what, the answer is that *"God's plan in history* has creation as its starting point" (pp. 139-140). Therefore, "creation being a commencement has a sequel;" that is, its sequel in history. But "creation which has a commencement and a history has also an end;" that is, it is as Ludwig Koehler has said, "an eschatological conception" (p. 142). Cosmological, historical, eschatological: these are the three theological facets of our Hebrew-Christian heritage of the concept of creation.

A more *philosophical* interpretation of creation is given by Claude Tresmontant in *A Study of Hebrew Thought.* His argument is that creation is the fundamental difference between Hebrew and Greek thought. Metaphysical language is not always easy to understand; but it is at least possible to sense something of the difference as Tresmontant states it: "Hebrew thought runs in a direction opposite to the current of Greek thought, mounts the slope which the Greeks and their followers descend, since the latter deem all tangible stuff to be born *from a decline,* a deg-

22

radation, while the Hebrew considers it the result *of an ascent,* the result of a truly positive act: creation." John M. Oesterreicher puts it more simply in the Foreword to Aresmontant's book; "the great metaphysical truth with which Tresmontant begins his study is the one that opens the Bible: The visible world is created." That is, it is not co-eternal with the living God. It is the result of an act of God. The distinction between the Creator and the creation is kept clear. As Oesterreicher rightly says, "Compared with the Platonic view of the world, this is a revolutionary doctrine." And it belong to our Hebrew-Christian heritage.

One thing more needs to be said to show the uniqueness of the biblical account of creation. There were other traditions concerning the creation of the world, especially among Israel's neighbors such as Sumer, Babylon, and Egypt; and it must be admitted that they too had a religious character. There is a Babylonian creation story *whose format* strongly resembles the biblical six-day week of Genesis 1. There are striking similarities between the two; and yet, as G. A. Barton points out in *Archaeology and the Bible,* and many others with him, the differences are even greater. The clarity and consistency of the biblical account contrasts sharply with the disordered confusion of the Babylonian. Furthermore the Babylonian story is mythological and polytheistic in character, with the gods represented as quarreling and fighting with each other, whereas the biblical story reflects *the most exalted monotheism.* To quote G. A. Barton, "The One God moves with a majestic aloneness through the activities of the creation week, unhelped and unhindered by any associate or rebel." John Oesterreicher goes even further and calls the Genesis account of creation "a new and happy message, a gospel." That is, we see *the love of God* in creation as well as in redemption; and above all, we see that *a created universe is a meaningful universe.* Such is the significance of creation in our Hebrew-Christian heritage according to those who have studied it carefully, as a concept and as an act of God.

Analysis of Genesis 1

Let us now look carefully at the *first* of the two creation stories with which Genesis begins. The *second* we shall examine in our next chapter, in connection with the doctrine of Man.

1. Introduction

By way of introduction let us attempt a general characterization of the section from Genesis 1: 1 to 2: 3; for it is within such a perspective that the details will assume their proper place and proportion in our interpretation of them.

First, then, this observation: that Genesis 1 is *a general account* of creation, *with a conscious symmetry* of literary construction or design. From the literary point of view, it is *panoramic* rather than annalistic in character. The emphasis is on *perspective* and relationship of parts, and on *general principles* rather than on annalistic details. It is like a picture, where you get the truest effect *if you see the whole* rather than give too close and critical scrutiny to minor details. The details are not unimportant, but they can be exaggerated out of all proportion if we fail to see their purpose in the light of the literary form as a whole.

Second, the primary purpose of the narrative is *religious* rather than scientific; although in dealing with the subject of the cosmos there is naturally a point of meeting between the two. It is indeed a biblical cosmology, but it is not written in scientific terms nor with a scientific purpose. Because of *its central religious purpose,* coupled with the fact that it is in a literary sense a general or a panoramic account, correct interpretation must stress *the major principles from a religious point of view.* As we shall see, this is exactly what our Hebrew-Christian heritage has done.

Third, the basic religious truth to be stressed is this, that *God created.* It is a truth quite as important in what it reveals concerning our God as it is in respect to the origin of the world. The First Article of the Apostles' Creed has unerringly put its finger on that which is of primary importance when it says, "I believe in God the Father Almighty, Maker of heaven and earth." But clustered around this central truth of *an act of God* are others which are also religiously significant.

With this general Introduction we proceed to a rather careful analysis of Genesis 1.

2. The Keynote

The keynote is found in the opening sentence; and what a sublime keynote it is! The Bible begins in the beginning *with God.* It does not begin with an argument that there is a God. It begins with the assertion that *God created,* and that he is therefore the beginning of all things. It may not assert, but it very definitely implies, that all that exists must be viewed and interpreted in their original and fundamental relationship to God as Creator. The truth to be stressed, therefore is this the *God created;* and the emphasis can be either on the noun or on the verb: for without saying a word as to the existence or the nature of God, it reveals a God who is personal and powerful, and who works with creative purpose and design. *The theology of Genesis 1 is as important as the cosmology.* "The sentences of chapter 1 are primarily declaration of faith," says Gerhard von Rad in his *Commentary on Genesis.* It is as a Confession of Faith that Genesis 1 has become a part of our Hebrew-Christian heritage; and this Confession centers in an act of God, it declares that the living God is in action as the Creator, it reveals a faith that concerns the existence of men here and now and in all eternity. How do we know that this is true? There is but one answer: the answer most clearly stated in Hebrews 11: 5, *"By faith* we understand that the world was created by the word of God, so that what is seen was made out of things which do not appear." In our Hebrew-Christian heritage creation is a faith to be proclaimed, not a truth to be proved.

3. The Key Verb

In what we have said about God acting in creation, we have already skirted the key verb of the chapter, the Hebrew *bara.* It is this verb which is always translated *create,* although it is roughly but not exactly synonymous with two other verbs, *make* and *form.* The uniqueness of *bara* is best expressed by this definition from the *Westminster Dictionary of the Bible,* "the verb always has God for its subject, and the result is an entirely new thing." Gerhard von Rad expands on this definition when he says in his *Commentary on Genesis,* "It means a creative activity, which in principle is without analogy. It is correct to say that the verb 'bara,' 'create,' contains the idea both of complete effortlessness and *creatio ex nihilo,* since it is never connected with any statment of the material. The hidden pathos of this statement is that God is the Lord of the world" (p. 47). The verb occurs especially in the Pentateuch and in Isaiah. It occurs three times in Genesis 1; which W. H. Turton, in *The Truth of Christianity* (1925), links with matter (vs. 1), mind (vs. 21), and spirit (vs. 27). Alternating as it does with the verb *made* the uniqueness given by definition to *bara* might certainly indicate these three especially significant points in the creative activity of God, something *new.* Yet, *all* is created; or as Luther puts it, "I believe that God has created me and all that exists."

4. In the Beginning

When we consider the phrase "in the beginning" we must remember that only God is from eternity. It is therefore a mistake to think of the beginning of creation in purely temporal terms. What is stressed by the writer of Genesis is simply the beginning of the creative work of God, undated and undateable. The RSV footnote probably gives the correct interpretation, the real meaning, of the phrase with the translation, "When God began to create." Christian faith is far less concerned with *the time* than it is with *the fact* of creation.

5. Cosmos versus Chaos

The second verse of Genesis 1 seems to indicate an ordering of a "cosmos" out of "chaos," which is a mythological concept. There is nevertheless a sharp demarcation between Israel's use of "cosmological and theogonic myths" and that of her heathen neighbors. To Israel God was *the Creator* and not simply one who subjected "a pre-existing chaos to his ordering will" (von Rad). Whatever the literary format, we can never escape this dominant note of *creation* in our Hebrew-Christian heritage, the note suggested by the unique Hebrew verb *bara*. See, by way of confirmation, Hebrews 11:3. However, this primary emphasis on creation in the sense of "a new thing" does not rule out the other impression given in the Genesis narrative that the created universe, of which man is a part, is *a cosmos* (suggesting order) rather than *a chaos* (suggesting confusion). How orderly this universe is has been demonstrated again and again by the exactitude of our space explorations, as well as by such simple experiences as that of night following day. Our God is a God of order, and the world which he has made reflects this orderliness in countless ways.

6. The Seven Days

The same can be said about the seven-day creative week which constitutes the format of the first creation story in Genesis. It is a literary form with conscious symmetry, so as to give a panoramic picture of *progression* and *order* in the creative process and result. It is only when we exaggerate details that belong to the literary form, and are therefore religiously unimportant, that religion and science really come into conflict. N. H. Ridderbos, in a book titled *Is There a Conflict Between Genesis 1 and Natural Science?*, refers to this "artificial arrangement" of Genesis 1 as the "framework hypothesis." It is an apt description. It is not the intent of the author, says Ridderbos, to present an exact report of what happened; but by placing the eightfold work of God within the framework of the six work days, plus a seventh day of rest, he succeeds as only a literary artist could do in stressing the all-important truth that God is the Creator of all that exists, and the equally important fact that the work of creation is complete and good in the sight of God. We may with von Rad see another purpose with this literary format of a series of days as drawing a line between the biblical account and every form of mythical thinking (Commentary on Genesis, p. 63). Karl Barth calls it an "historical reality," even though it is outside of the reach of all historical observation and report. It is *the reality* of creation as an act of God that is fundamental to our Hebrew-Christian heritage.

7. The Use of Hebrew Singular-Collective Nouns

It is of some significance that every reference from verse 11 on to plants, fruit trees, swarms of living creatures, birds, cattle, creeping things, and beasts of the earth, employs in the original Hebrew what we call a singular-collective noun. It is significant because it indicates that the creation story in Genesis 1 embraces *the totality* of life down through the ages. Must not the same be true of the word for *man, adam* (vs. 26-27)? The reference would seem to be to man in the sense of "all men" or "Everyman," or of humanity. In another context *adam* might indeed represent a single man, Adam, but not in the panoramic perspective of the creation story in Genesis 1. Again we refer to Luther as having caught the essential meaning of our Hebrew-Christian heritage when he says, "I believe that God has created *me* (and therefore surely *Everyman*) and all that exists."

8. Man in the Image of God

This brings us to the second most important feature of the narrative in Genesis 1, the climactic position of *man*. The first, of course, is the unique confession of faith in God as the Creator. We shall have more to say of Man in our next chapter, from another perspective than here. At the moment we are concerned with the meaning and interpretation of the phrase "in the image of God," for this is certainly essential both to the creation story in Genesis 1 and to our Hebrew-Christian heritage. It is a phrase which has been variously interpreted, though the interpretations are not necessarily mutually exclusive.

One way to define it is in terms of *personality*, or what Helmut Thielicke calls "the gift of personhood," which differentiates man from all other creatures. One writer has said that "Personality involves three things: self-consciousness, reasoning power, and moral sense. In other words, any being that can say to himself: 'I am, I ought, I will,' is made in the image of God." (Albertus Pieters, *Notes on Genesis*). The fact that man, and man alone, is such a creature is sufficient to explain the climactic position of the account of his creation in the total confession of faith in Genesis 1.

But it is also possible to define the image of God in terms of *character*. This is what the *Augustana Catechism* (1939) does, when it says: "God created man in his own image, so that he was sinless and blessed." The Apology of the Augsburg Confession defines the image of God in the context of original sin as the lack of original righteousness: "What else is this than that a wisdom and righteousness was implanted in man that would grasp God and reflect him, that is, that man received gifts like the the knowledge of God, fear of God, and trust in God?" (*The Book of Concord,* Tappert's edition, 1959, pp. 102-103.) Such an interpretation seems to be supported by Paul's words in Eph. 5: 9 and Col. 3: 10, which describe *renewal* in the image of God as involving the knowledge of God, righteousness, and truth. There is of course nothing to hinder us from seeing *both personality and character* in the image of God. As E. F. Kevan says in *The New Bible Commentary* (p. 73), "This likeness is both natural and moral, in the possession of personality and character." The two are not mutually exclusive. This was the viewpoint of such Lutheran theologians as C. E. Lindberg, Henry Eyster Jacobs, and Jacob Tanner. This is also the viewpoint of our Hebrew-Christian heritage. Nor does this combination exclude still another possible facet of interpretation, that the image of God refers to man as *God's representative,* appointed by God to exercise *dominion* in the earth.

There is a third definition of the image of God, and that is in terms of a unique *relationship* to God, or of a capacity for fellowship which belongs to man alone. Herbert C. Alleman, in the *Alleman-Flack Old Testament Commentary,* connects *personality* with *covenant*: "Personality for the Hebrews was the first attribute of their God. Man is related to God by a spiritual bond from the very manner of his creation. His creation is a covenant relationship." (pp. 174-174). We shall have more to say about *covenant* in a later chapter. For the moment the word *relationship* may suffice. As Claus Westermann has said about the image of God (in *A Thousand Years and a Day,* 1962) : "This means that God created man to be in a personal relationship with himself." He continues: "Man is God's likeness insofar as he may listen to God and talk to him, humble himself before God and praise him. The other side of this message is this: human existence can only find fulfillment in personal relationship with God. A man who no longer has a personal relationship with God is no longer a man." (pp. 9-10). Dietrich Bonhoeffer, in *Creation and Fall* (Eng. tr.

28

1959), also speaks of the image as a relationship between two persons, a relationship of *freedom,* in which man is created free to worship God and to serve the neighbor (p. 35). Personality, character, dominion, relationship, freedom, worship, service: all are different facets or aspects of the image of God in our Hebrew-Christian heritage.

9. The Sabbath

The concluding note in the first Genesis creation story has reference to the seventh day or the sabbath (Gen. 2: 1-3). The seventh day is marked by divine resting rather than by creative activity. How sharply shall we construe this rest from creative activity? It certainly does not mean that God has ceased to be *a God who acts.* We remember the words of Jesus, "My Father is working still, and I am working" (Jn. 5: 17). One phase of his activity in relation to the universe was finished, but his work goes on. It is significant, as von Rad has pointed out, that *God finished his work on the seventh day* rather than on the sixth, and that this day has no termini of "evening" and "morning" as do the others. It is as if the author were suggesting that God acts and rests at the same time. There is no direct connection of the seventh day and the Hebrew sabbath in the creation story, but the two are linked in the Decalog (Exodus 20) where the sabbath as a day of rest unto the Lord is motivated by God's resting from his creative acts. An eschatological application is given in the New Testament, in Hebrews 4. "This rest is in every respect a new thing," says Gerhard von Rad, and is "a rest that existed before man and still exists without man's perceiving it."

Other Bible References to Creation

We shall have more to say about the image of God in our next chapter when we discuss the doctrine of Man. At that time we will also give careful study to the second Genesis creation story, in chapters 2 and 3. Before we conclude this chapter let us ask: how general is the doctrine of creation elsewhere in the Bible?

We must admit that there is no biblical reference to the literary format of Genesis 1, the six creative days; or to what Ridderbos calls *the framework hypothesis.* Putting it in another way, there is no direct reference to a creative *process* or to *an exact cosmology,* as some who take everything in the Bible with exact literalness would interpret Genesis 1.

On the other hand, there are many significant references to *the theology* of Creation, to the relationship between *God as Creator* (Maker) *and Man as creature,* and to the demands of this relationship on Man, as well as the comfort and hope that it gives. Less frequent, but still significant, are the references to God as Creator of the universe, or of all that exists.

We shall single out for attention just a few of the references to creation outside of Genesis.

There is the admonition in Ecclesiastes 12: 1-7, "Remember also your Creator in the days of your youth, before the evil days come —," that is, before life ends in death.

According to Psalm 95: 6-7 the fact that the Lord is our Maker should lead to humble, confident worship. This is also the climactic note in Luther's explanation of the First Article: "Therefore I surely ought to thank and praise, serve and obey him."

In Isaiah 40: 12-31, one of the truly great passages in the Old Testament, the God of creation is presented as also the God of redemptive history. The conclusion of the prophet can be summed up with these words: What confidence this thought, this knowledge, this faith, should inspire!

Israel's grievous sin, according to the prophet Hosea, was that she so often *forgot* her Maker and trusted in her own strength and in lifeless idols unable to help. See, for example, Hosea 2: 13 and 8: 4.

Malachi 2: 10 teaches *the universal fatherhood* of God as the Creator of all, of which the corollary naturally is *the universal brotherhood* of Man. These are two wonderful concepts of our Hebrew-Christian heritage; which must be handled with care lest they be wrongly applied, but which dare certainly not be shunned by the Christian. There is one sense in which we are all children of God by virtue of creation, and another and more intimate sense in which we may be his children by virtue of redemption and personal faith in the Redeemer. If this seems to be a paradox the explanation will come as we study the second creation story in Genesis and follow through with the biblical doctrine of Man as he is today.

Two New Testament passages concerning creation are certainly a part of our Hebrew-Christian heritage according to the Christian interpretation. In Romans 1: 18-25 *all* are held to be without excuse if they exchange the will and worship of God the Creator for idolatry and all kinds of lustful sins. On the very basis of creation men ought to know that *God is* and that he deserves to be praised and served. In I Peter 4: 19 we have this encouraging admonition, "Therefore let those who suffer according to God's will do right and entrust their souls to a faithful creator."

These two passages look backward to God's act of creation at the beginning. There is also, however, a continuing creative activity whereby in Christ the believer becomes "a new creation" or "a new creature" (II Cor. 5: 17), having put on "the new nature, which is being renewed in knowledge after the image of its creator" (Cor. 3: 10). Of this spiritual new creation we shall have more to say later. For the moment what we have said must suffice. There cannot be the slightest doubt that the doctrine of creation was fundamental both to the Hebrew and to the Christian faith. In our next chapter, on the basis of the second Genesis creation story, we shall search more deeply into its significance in relation to the doctrine of Man.

In a sermon based on the First Article of the Apostles' Creed, Martin Luther admits that there are many things about creation that are difficult to understand (*Genom tron allena*, an anthology of Luther's sermons, edited by Kjell-Ove Nilsson, 1967). With this we will readily agree. Let us also admit that it does not profit much in preaching and teaching to probe deeply into these difficult things. Let us say rather with Luther, "For us it is enough if we can believe in creation as *a work of God.*" This is also the heart of the doctrine of creation in our Hebrew-Christian heritage of faith.

Chapter 3

THE HEBREW-CHRISTIAN CONCEPT OF MAN

Edmond Jacob, the Old Testament biblical theologian, has said that "Everything the Old Testament has to teach about man can be found in the narratives of the Creation"; that is, in the first few chapters of Genesis. (*A Companion to the Bible,* art. Man). This is essentially true, though the New Testament contributes much to the deepening of our knowledge of man. In this chapter we shall concentrate on Genesis 2-4 as our chief Bible reading; that is, on the second creation narrative in Genesis, which is different from the first in literary format and in theological purpose, but whose teaching is supplementary rather than contradictory to that of Genesis 1.

The interrelationship between the first three topics in our study of our Hebrew-Christian heritage can be simply shown. It is a relationship between God the Creator and Man the creature on the basis of creation as an act of God. It is within this relationship that we learn to know what really matters concerning both God and Man. The Bible seldom speaks of the one apart from the other.

Genesis 1: 26-27: A Review

Review is always in order, and never more so than here. What did this passage teach us concerning the nature of Man? We remember the panoramic character of Genesis 1, which gives us a picture of the creation of the world, with Man in the climactic position. We remember from the consistent use of singular-collective nouns that here "Adam is Everyman" or humanity. We remember also the uniqueness of the creation of Man, in the image of God. We remember the various interpretations of this unique phrase, which together give us a clear biblical picture of Man: endowed with personality, or personhood, "a reasonable and moral creature," who can say to himself, "I am, I ought, I will;" endowed with character, with wisdom and righteousness, with sinlessness and blessedness, or with such gifts as the knowledge of God, the fear of God, confidence in God, and the like; endowed with a likeness to God which was both "natural and moral," including both personality and character, and qualifying him both for the role of dominion over God's world and for a special relationship with God himself. As we have already pointed out, none of these are mutually exclusive. My own primary emphasis is on man's unique *relationship* to God, which rests on his personhood and is directed towards the role of dominion in the earth and of worship and praise of God and of service in love towards the neighbor. Speaking in ideal terms, such was the role of man as God created him. That man today does not measure up to this ideal is another matter, which we shall discuss as we go along. On the basis of Genesis 1: 26-27, however, certain statements may be made, and have been made, that are of fundamental significance to our Hebrew-Christian heritage.

For example, St. Augustine in his Confessions makes this illuminating statement concerning God and Man: "Thou awakest us to delight in Thy praise; for Thou madest us for Thyself, and our heart is restless, until it repose in Thee."

We have already noticed Luther's existential interpretation, when he says: "I believe that God has created *me*." Each human life is a gift from God. Each human life is meant to be a personal relationship with God. It is a continuing relationship of preservation, provision, and protection. Creation and Providence are inseparable. Moreover, as Creator, God acts purely in goodness and mercy, without merit or worthiness in me. Nevertheless there is a response expected, a duty enjoined upon me, because of this Creator-creature relationship: "wherefore I am in duty bound to thank and praise, serve and obey him." This religious aspect of creation is a fundamental part of our Hebrew-Christian heritage, far more important than any merely biological aspect; though that, as we shall see, belongs to the complete picture.

Alan Richardson has enlarged upon Luther's theme in his little *Commentary on Genesis I-XI:* "Unless I know that I am created by God, am utterly dependent upon him, am responsible to him and judged by him, the creation of the world will be for me only a philosophical speculation —. To know that God made *me* (and *therefore* all the world) is to understand the parables of Creation aright; it is this kind of 'existential' knowledge which the Genesis stories of Creation can communicate to us or awaken in us. When they do so — when I can say that they are true *for me* — then I know that God has spoken his word to me through them, and they are indeed for me *sacred* scriptures." (p. 43). Such is our Hebrew-Christian heritage of faith.

Along the same line, although his point of departure may seem to be Genesis 2: 7 rather than Genesis 1: 26-27, Helmut Thielicke (in *How the World Began*) correctly says: "You cannot define man on the basis of his biological origin; you must define him in the light of his destiny, his goal." (p. 84). Man's creation in the image of God implies a present spiritual relationship between the two; or at least a capacity for such a relationship. It also implies, as Ludwig Kohler has said, a future eschatological goal. It is significant to note that whether it be the philosopher Tresmontant, or the theologian Bonhoeffer, or the Nobel scientist Sir John Eccles, "the peculiar relationship of man and God" is both defended and proclaimed. Of course, none of these men would deny biological evolution up to a point; but all of them would emphatically affirm that biological evolution does not tell "the ultimate story" (Eccles) concerning my origin as a person, my self-awareness and personality, and the possibility of my unique relationship with God. It is this fact of a unique relationship with God because created in his image that constitutes the heart of our Hebrew-Christian heritage. As we quoted earlier from Claus Westermann, "A man who no longer has a personal relationship with God is no longer a man": not in the true sense of the word. Whether all men believe it or not, such was the ancient Hebrew confession of faith, such is still the Christian confession of faith, such is historically our Hebrew-Christian heritage.

Genesis 2: A Parallel Confession

The second affirmation concerning Man in our Hebrew-Christian heritage is based on Genesis 2: 7, the key-verse to the second creation narrative.

The second creation narrative differs from the first in several significant ways. Whereas the first narrative is a panoramic picture of the cosmos (or universe) and of man's place in it, the second is a more detailed story of the origin, nature, environment, and early experience of Man. We might call it indeed the Story of Man, which is essentially the story that the Bible aims to tell. The second narrative is also markedly anthropomorphic in character; that is, God's actions in relation to man are described as if he were himself a man. This is not an unusual story device in the Old Testament, nor does it in any way affect the truth of the story; it does, of course, affect the interpretation. Then too the order of events

34

is different in the two creation narratives; so that we must look to *theology* and *purpose* if we are to see how they complement rather than contradict each other.

The key-verse, as we have said, is Genesis 2: 7. "Then the LORD God formed man of dust from the ground, and breathed into his nostrils the breath of life; and man became a living being."

We observe that the verb now is not "created" but "formed." The imagery also is different: instead of a creation "ex nihilo" we have now a formation "of dust." The precise manner in which God formed man "dust from the ground" is not spelled out. It might have been as a sculptor molding clay, but it does not say so. It might have been instantaneously, with a single spoken word, but it does not say so. It might have been through a long history of biological evolution, as many devout Christian scholars today believe: see how carefully Helmut Thielicke handles this question in *How the World Began,* pp. 79-80, 82-83; but again we must confess that Genesis 2: 7 does not say so. The question of "the mode" is left unanswered, except that it is clearly seen as an act of God. The important question is not "whence man came" but rather "why is he here."

Theologically speaking, in terms of religious faith, Genesis 2: 7 tells us three things:

It tells us that from one aspect of his nature man is earth-related. The formation of his body "of dust from the ground" implies that man is mortal, and that he will again return to dust. This fact that man's body is connected with the dust could of course be discovered without divine revelation; what is "revealed" is the fact that God made him so. Moreover, this earth-relatedness of man suggests that physically he is dependent on his earthly environment for "food and raiment" and for all material good. As touching his bodily life he stands in daily need of what this earth provides under the power of God, and he is in duty bound to thank and praise God who "daily provides abundantly for all the needs of his life."

Another thing to which Genesis 2: 7 bears witness is the unique God-relatedness of man, because God himself "breathed into his nostrils the breath of life." This inbreathed breath of life is comparable in significance to the image of God in Genesis 1: 26-27. It suggests the unique relation of dependence on and responsibility to God. Man has a spiritual as well as a physical nature. He has received from God a spirit as well as a body, and this gift of the spirit implies the potential for immortality;

as the Preacher says in Ecclesistes 12 : 7, "and the dust returns to the earth as it was, and the spirit returns to God who gave it."

The third significant thing affirmed in Genesis 2 : 7 is that of the *wholeness of man*. Man *has* a body and a *spirit*, but he *is* a living being. It is true that there is a physical as well as a psychical aspect of his nature; or shall we say that the material and the spiritual combine to make him what he is: a total person, a unified being. There is no sharp dichotomy between soul (mind) and body (matter) as in Greek thought. Our Hebrew-Christian heritage thinks of man as one unified living being, who possesses *a wholeness* in which spirit and body, his God-relatedness and his earth-relatedness are intimately bound together in one wonderfully complex *being* or *person*. This wholeness of man sheds light on some problems, such as the psychosomatic character of much illness and other human experiences. It is also a wonderful source of comfort to know that God care for me *as a person*, and that he is concerned to provide abundantly for both my material and spiritual needs. In Genesis 2 it is the garden which is the symbol of God's abundant, gracious provision for the physical side of man's life. In Genesis 3, as we shall see, it is the picture of *the seeking God* which becomes a symbol and expression of God's similar concern for the spiritual side of man's life. But in actual human experience the two are never separated, for God deals with man as a living being, and his concern is for man in his wholeness. This wholeness of man does raise a question as to what happens when we die. Does it imply *that the whole man dies,* that we cease to exist? This is the thought-pattern of some modern theologians, but definitely not of our Hebrew-Christian heritage. To give such an interpretation would contradict not only the verse from Ecclesiastes 12 : 7 previously quoted, but also the unanimous testimony of the New Testament. "Therefore, if any one is in Christ, he is a new creation (RSV footnote, a new creature) :" and we may rightly ask, Can I ever cease to be what I am in Christ? "The free gift of God is eternal life in Christ Jesus our Lord (Rom. 6 : 23) :" it is ours as a gift, behind which stands the faithful and firm word of God. We shall have more to say about the theological debate concerning the immortality of the soul versus the resurrection of the dead in a later chapter. At the moment we are concerned to forestall any wrong conclusions from the wonderful teaching of our Hebrew-Christian heritage concerning the wholeness of man. Let us use it rather as a strong encouragement to faith in God our Creator who is concerned with us in all our needs. Jesus spoke with this same reassuring faith to his disciples in the sermon on the mount (Mt. 6: 25-33). Our heavenly Father knows that we need food and drink and clothes, and has promised to provide what we need; but he knows also that our greatest need is for the righteousness that qualifies us to enter into his kingdom, and for this too he has made provision through Christ.

Actually there is no essential difference between the Doctrine of Man in Genesis 2: 7 and in Genesis 1: 26-27. Both stress the existence of a unique personal relationship between Man as a creature and God as his Maker. Both Genesis 1 and Genesis 2 stress God's gracious provision for man's material needs; both assign him a position of dominion, not in his own right but as God's representative, within God's overall creation. The wholeness of man is implied in the first creation story and clearly stated in the second; but it is in the second that the *mortality* of man, of which we shall have more to say later, becomes clearly evident. It is in the second also that we have a clear symbolic reference to *obedience* to the will of God *as the test* of a right spiritual relationship to the living God as man's Creator. Of this too we shall have more to say shortly.

Genesis 2: 18-25: Man and Woman

The second chapter of Genesis closes with a vivid anthropomorphic account of the creation of Woman. This too is an essential part of our Hebrew-Christian heritage concerning the concept of man. In Genesis 1: 27 we have simply the statement, "male and female he created them." In Genesis 2 the relationship between Man and Woman is set forth in greater detail. Woman was created to be *a helper* to Man. That does not mean servanthood, which could have been found in the animal world, but equality. Furthermore, the statement that "they became one flesh" suggests not only sexuality, leading to procreation, but the unity of love in every area of married life. The most significant word, of course, is *helper*. From the negative point of view there was no "helper fit for him" to be found among the animals, who were created for a subordinate position. From the positive point of view God created Woman to be "a helper fit for him." With the creation of Woman came the establishment of marriage and the home, the first of the basic social units to be established among men. According to the confession of faith recorded here it was established on the basis of monogamy, in purity and innocence. It is true that polygamy was practiced at times in the Old Testament world, especially during the monarchy, and was not formally condemned by either Moses or the prophets; but it is clear from Genesis 2 that monogamy was regarded as the ideal form of marriage. The New Testament knows of no other form. There are some beautiful instances of family life in the Bible, and the emphasis on the family has been perpetuated among both Jews and Christians. It is still one of the precious concepts of our Hebrew-Christian heritage, even if some unfortunately have failed to grasp the full impact of what a home is meant to be, and under God can be: a place of helpfulness and of equality in mutual love. There is a fine Christian interpretation of God's intent as to the relationship between husband and wife in Ephesians 5: 21-23, where it is likened to that between Christ and the Church. Needless to say there is no sanction in the Hebrew-Christian tradition for abnormal sex acts of any kind. The Pauline epistles in the New Testament are particularly strong and straightforward in their denunciation of such acts as belonging to "the works of the flesh," from which Christ has set us free. But at this juncture, before we reach the story of fallen man in Genesis 3, the very suggestion that such acts might occur seems strangely out of place. When God created Man and Woman in his own image, for a unique personal relationship with himself, there was nothing in this other relation between the two of them as Man and Wife of which they needed to be ashamed. The sense of shame came later as a result of sin.

Genesis 3: Test, Temptation, Fallen Man

Genesis 3 is a most significant chapter in Bible history! It is this chapter rather than Genesis 1 that gives the real key to the narrative that follows; and without this chapter the whole Bible, in its history and in its theology, becomes meaningless. It is against its dark background that we can understand the state of the world as it is, as well as the story of God's redemptive purpose and activity which, far more than creation, is the theme of the Bible and the central message of our Hebrew-Christian heritage. This will become clear in succeeding chapters. Right now we are concerned with the characterization of man as a sinner, in need of salvation. What has happened to man who was created with a unique capacity for fellowship with God?

From Genesis 2: 16-17 we learn that the very nature of man's unique relationship with his Maker subjected him to the test of obedience. The symbol of the tree "of the knowledge of good and evil" may seem mysterious, but does it not really tell us a very simple but profound truth: that God alone has the authority to say what is good and what is evil, and that man has no right to arrogate this authority to himself; he is in duty bound to obey the will of God and to submit to his Word.

But from Genesis 3 we observe how this test of obedience, which is inherent in the very relationship between man and God, became a temptation to disobedience. Who made it so? Not God! There is a fundamental biblical statement about temptation in James 1: 13, 14: "God cannot be tempted with evil and he himself tempts no one." What Genesis 3 tells us is that there is a spiritual tempter who can turn a divine test into temptation by putting a different construction on the same set of facts. What makes the difference? The purpose of a test is that a man may stand, and be stronger for the testing; the purpose of temptation is that he may fall, and be spiritually and morally defeated. The same situation in life may be a test or a temptation according as it is seen from God's or from Satan's point of view, or interpretation. So it was in the beginning, and so it is now.

If we would know and be warned of the steps in temptation as understood by our Hebrew-Christian heritage there is no better teacher than the story in Genesis 3. How true it is to temptation as we know it today, in our own experience, or from observation!

It is first a temptation to doubt (vs. 1). It may be doubt of God's word, or of his goodness, or of both. Can a prohibition be "good"? Man still thinks along that line. But the basic question concerns God himself, or the truth of his Word. *"Did* God say;" does God say: the real test of obedience and the temptation to disobedience rests right here. If we trust his word we will obey his will. The first human pair did not. The same is all too often true of man today.

The moment man shows himself susceptible to doubt the tempter follows with outright denial of God's word as set forth in his test. The denial is directed especially at God's warning of what would happen if they disobeyed. Disobedience will not bring death: instead it will open the way to greatness, like unto that of God himself. "For God knows that when you eat of it your eyes will be opened, and you will be like God, knowing good and evil." The temptation was to put man on a level with God. Ever so subtly the denial is mingled with deceit: God's loving purpose for man is denied; he is pictured as holding back something good lest man become his equal. Don't get hung up on the fact that this story is in the form of a parable, wherein are some things hard to understand. The essential truth of the story, the nature of temptation then and now, comes through clearly enough. It is true today. Doubt, leading to denial of God's word, culminating in a growing desire or lust for the forbidden ambition of becoming the arbiter of what is good and evil, the temptation to make man instead of God the center of the universe: is not this the story of man down through the ages, and in our own day? Leander S. Keyser has pointed out in his book called *Man's First Disobedience* that the first temptation was threefold in its appeal: first, chiefly physical; second, physico-psychical in almost equal ratio; third, mainly psychical. He adds, "We know of no other way by which moral tests come to man." The underlying reason for this is wholeness of man of which we spoke in connection with Genesis 2: 7. A vivid confirmation of its truth is to be found in the threefold temptation of Jesus (Mt. 4). If further confirmation were needed it is supplied by the summary statement in I John 2: 16, "For all that is in the world, the lust of the flesh and the lust of the eyes and the pride of life, is not of the Father but is of the world. "

Whatever the steps in temptation it ended in the disaster of disobedience to the will of God. Man sinned against his Maker, and thereby altered fundamentally the unique relationship with God implicit in his creation in God's own image. It is not the teaching of our Hebrew-Christion heritage that man lost all capacity for such a relationship. He did not cease to be a person. Nevertheless something happened to him that changed the whole course of human history. We can no longer speak of man as being essentially good. He became a sinner by his act of disobedience; for though the word "sin" does not occur here, the fact of disobedience does: and disobedience on the part of man to the will of God is sin. It makes no difference that many people today, including some theologians, do not like to hear about sin or to admit its existence. It stares us in the face in the story of Man as the Bible tells it. The doctrine of man as a sinner in need of salvation from outside himself is essential to our Hebrew-Christian heritage. For a generation that prides itself on "telling things as they are" the refusal to recognize the reality of sin in human existence seems strangely irrelevant and inconsistent. George A. Buttrick has described the situation so accurately in *Christ and Man's Dilemma:* "We are ignorant. We are wicked. We are mortal." This is what we mean by the Fall. Man by his act of willful disobedience *lost* what the Lutheran Confessions refer to as the (true) knowledge of God, the (right) fear of God, and the (trusting) confidence in God. He became alienated from God, and often at enmity with him. In its simplest terms the Bible story tells us that man fled from God in fear and shame. If the relationship thus broken was ever to be reestablished it would require a new act of God, who had first acted in creation.

Genesis 3: R *ff: The Seeking God*

Into this situation of man's making the Lord God came (and comes) to seek man out where he tries to hide himself "from the presence" of God. If we are to understand what our Hebrew-Christian heritage teaches concerning Man we must also understand what it teaches about the seeking God. How do you read the story in Genesis 3? For what reason did God come to ask the question, "Where are you?" What is his continuing concern with Man? To be specific, does he come in grace or in wrath, for purposes of judgment or of salvation? The answer follows in all the rest of the Bible.

God does indeed come to pronounce judgment: on the tempter, on woman, on man, on the very earth for man's sake. Death, which was included as a warning note in the original test of obedience, becomes a threatening reality. The New Testament puts it succinctly: "The wages of sin is death."

But it would be a caricature of God if we were to think of him as coming simply to say, "I told you so," and then to confirm the sentence of death. The very fact that God is concerned enough about man to seek him out in his fallen condition is a ray of hope, which indicates that he acts in grace. There is a clear continuity of theological principle between *the seeking God* in Genesis and the New Testament declaration by Jesus, "For the Son of man came to seek and to save that which was lost." In the very moment of man's utter defeat *God acts* in grace and love to renew the conflict with the tempter; and there is at least a hint in Genesis 3: 15, which by some has been called *the first Gospel promise,* of ultimate victory in the conflict. From here on the themes of judgment and of redemption alternate in the Old Testament; but the primary emphasis, as we shall soon see, is on God as Redeemer. The New Testament makes this emphasis clearer still. It is a major concept, as we shall soon see, in our Hebrew-Christian heritage. For the moment we are concerned with Genesis 3. Here is portrayed, not the ideal man, but man as he is, a sinner, under judgment, and alienated from God; here is portrayed also the seeking God, who in righteousness condemns the sinner to death, but who in grace and mercy seeks the sinner's return and the renewal of the broken relationship established in creation. Enigmatic as the words in Genesis 3: 15 may seem to be (and perhaps must be at this stage of man's history and experience) the word is sure that the battle between the tempter and the tempted, between good and evil, is not ended in man's utter defeat; but rather *that God will act* to incite and to empower man for continuing con-

41

flict with evil, with hope of ultimate victory if in faith we choose to be on the side of God, or *to let God be with us*. This is the hope of our Hebrew-Christian heritage. God acts in redeeming love to seek and to save that which was lost. How does man respond? This is the story that begins to unfold from Genesis 4 on, and continues until we hear the word of him who sits upon the throne, "Behold, I make all things new" (Rev. 21: 5).

Genesis 4-11: The Two Ways

We began our study of the biblical concept of Man by noting the statement of Edmond Jacob, "Everything that the Old Testament has to teach about man can be found in the narratives of the Creation."

Before we conclude this study we must note one further affirmation concerning Man, in Genesis 4-11: an affirmation concerning *the two ways* set before him, and between which he must choose, whether it be Adam, or his descendants, or you and me, or Everyman.

The symbolic representatives of the two ways are Cain and Abel, and after him, Seth. In Jude 11 we are warned against walking "in the way of Cain." Putting together Hebrews 11: 4 and the story in Genesis, we may say it was a way marked by pride and self-righteousness and unbelief and violence and alienation from God. By contrast the way of Abel-Seth was marked by faith and true worship and a righteousness approved by God and by a devoted allegiance to God which, in the case of two of his descendants, Enoch, Genesis 5: 24, and Noah, Genesis 6: 9, is described as *a walk with God*. The more we read the more clearly we see that the division point between the two ways is *faith*. Or shall we say *obedience*? The two are so closely related in man's response to the divine seeking and saving will as to be almost inseparable.

Obedience to the will of God was at the heart of the test of man's relationship to the Creator. When man sinned it was through disobedience. There is only one way back to God and that is through obedience. But *whose* obedience? We shall have much more to say about that question later on. The answer ultimately is through Christ, who "became obedient unto death, even death on a cross" (Philippians 2:8), having "learned obedience through what he suffered" (Hebrews 5: 8), and "being made perfect he became the source of eternal salvation to all who obey him" (Hebrews 5: 9). *His* is the perfect obedience as the Son to the will of God the Father in our behalf, which as an act of God *reopens* the broken relationship. *Ours* is the obedience of faith which thankfully receives this new opportunity, this gift of renewed power, to do the will of God for which we were created. In Genesis we see this Way dimly foreshadowed. See the simple outline of The Two Ways appended to this chapter. In the New Testament we see the Way in clear perspective as disciples of Christ. It is the final consummation of our Hebrew-Christian heritage concerning the concept of Man in his relationship to God.

We conclude this chapter on the doctrine of Man by noting three things:

I. The shifting manner of reference to Man in the Old Testament, depending on which aspect the writer wished to emphasize. For instance, in Psalm 8 the psalmist meditates on the insignificance of man in himself and his greatness in the eyes of God. He is bold enough to say that "thou hast made him little less than God." From one point of view, looking at man's potential as God created him in his own image, this is true. On the other hand, in Psalm 49 the writer says that man is "like the beasts that perish." This also is true if we look at man simply in the experience of his mortality. Yet, in the same psalm the writer says,

> "But God will ransom my soul from the power of Sheol,
> for he will receive me."

The biblical concept of Man is not a simplistic one. That should already be apparent, and will become more so as we proceed.

II. While both Jews and Christians find a common heritage in the Old Testament there are also significant differences of interpretation, not least when it concerns what we call the Fall of man. The Christian understanding of the Old Testament teaching is clearly presented by Paul in Romans 5: 12-21. Read it carefully in the light of the narrative in Genesis 3. Then contrast it with this quotation from *The Pentateuch and Haftorahs*, edited by J. H. Hertz: "Instead of the Fall of man (in the sense of humanity as a whole), Judaism preaches the Rise of man; and instead of Original Sin, it stresses Original Virtue, the beneficent hereditary influence of righteous ancestors upon their descendants. — There is no loss of the God-likeness of man, nor of man's ability to do right in the eyes of God; and no such loss has been transmitted to his latest descendants. — Judaism clings to the idea of Progress." But this is not the teaching of our common Hebrew-Christian heritage as found in Genesis nor in the Old Testament as a whole. The Christian understanding of the concept of Fallen Man conforms much more closely to the teaching of the Scriptures, and indeed to human experience in a wicked world. Man is a sinner. Only God can save him from his sin.

43

III. Gerhard von Rad in his *Commentary on Genesis* summarizes the predicament of man in excellent fashion when he says, "The manifold, profound troubles in human life have their root in the *one* trouble of man's relationship to God." He adds by way of explanation, "Man was surrounded completely by God's providential goodness. But incomprehensibly he denied God obedience. Paradise is irreparably lost; what is left for man is a life of trouble in the shadow of a crushing riddle, a life entangled in an unbounded and completely hopeless struggle with the power of evil and in the end unavoidably subject to the majesty of death." So indeed it would have been for Everyman if it were not for the fact of *the seeking God*, who finally sent his only Son into the world to seek and to save that which was lost. To this signficant concept in our Hebrew-Christian heritage we look forward for further study.

THE TWO WAYS
Division Point — Genesis 3: 15

	Cain	Abel (Seth)
Cain	Eve's reaction at birth of	Seth

"I have gotten a man with the help of the LORD."
Gen. 4: 1

"God has appointed for me another child instead of Abel." Gen. 4: 25

Cain, Tiller of the Soil	Occupation	Abel, Shepherd
Fruit of the ground	Offering	Firstling of the Flock

Attitude
(Contrast suggested by Jude 11)

WAY OF CAIN	WAY OF ABEL
1. Evil — I Jn. 3: 12	1. Righteous — I Jn. 3: 12
2. Unbelief	2. Faith — Hebr. 11: 4

The Protevangelium

3. Sacrifice unacceptable	3. A more excellent sacrifice Hebr. 11: 4

Faith made the difference.

4. Worshipper, warned, rejected	4. Worshipper accepted
5. A persecutor, a murderer; wrong relation to God, to his brother.	5. An innocent sufferer — First martyr — Mt. 23 :35.

SELF-SATISFIED EARTH POSSESSORS	PILGRIMS IN FAITH

Developing:

A godless culture — Gen. 4: 16-24	Organized Yahweh worship — Gen. 4: 26

Illustrations:

1. City-builders	1. A walk with God, Enoch
2. Rampant wickedness under Lamech: bigamy, bloodshed, boasting pride.	2. Looked for a better city, country — Hebr. 11: 16 (10)

Kingdom of the World..............CONFLICT........................Kingdom of God

Satan's first blow against "the seed of the woman" —
Persecution (Cain, Abel)
Unsuccessful: kingdom of God survives persecution.
God raises up "another seed."

Satan's worst blow against the "seed of woman" —
Compromise; distinction breaks down — Gen. 6: 5.
Also unsuccessful: kingdom survives apostasy, syncretism.
separation through judgment: the Flood.

A NEW BEGINNING — NOAH — ABRAHAM.

Chapter 4

ELECTION, COVENANT, AND MISSION

Thus far we have studied three significant concepts in our Hebrew-Christian heritage: the doctrine of God, of Creation, and of Man. They are, as we have seen, closely interrelated and overlapping. Let us review briefly what we have seen, first in the form of a simple outline or diagram:

The Teaching Concerning		
GOD	CREATION	MAN
The living God	An act of God	In the image of God
A God who acts	A unique relationship	A sinner, fallen man, in need of redemption

We noted that Man, though created in the image of God and destined for a happy personal "I — Thou" relationship with his Maker, chose to disobey God, and through his unbelief and disobedience became alienated from God and came under his judgment; and that Everyman therefore stands in need of redemption and reconciliation, or of restoration to the lost image defined as unbroken relationship, something which only another act of God, the Seeking God, could provide. Romans 5: 12 interprets the human situation succinctly: "Therefore as sin came into the world through one man and death through sin, and so death spread to all men because all men sinned —."

We have already quoted George Buttrick's characterization of Man as he is, as the Bible portrays him, in *Christ and Man's Dilemma:* "Man is ignorant (that is, of God). Man is wicked. Man is mortal." At this juncture, it may be even more helpful to call attention to Gerhard von Rad's excellent summary of Genesis 3-11 in his *Commentary on Genesis,* pp. 149-150. His discussion is a prelude to the Call of Abraham in Genesis 12 ff., where we shall see clearly illustrated the threefold theme of this chapter: election, covenant, and mission. In the preceding chapters of Genesis von Rad notes an "increasing disturbance in the relationship between humanity and God," as well as "progressive divine judgment" and "continued divine preservation." Of special significance is the culminating judgment "on the nations," as well as the still unanswered question about God's salvation for all nations. The answer to this latter question is given most unexpectedly, says von Rad, in "the particularism of election," the choosing of one man, Abraham, and of one people, Israel, to the seeming exclusion of all others.

This brings us to the story of Abraham, and to the themes of election, covenant, and mission so closely related to that story.

Genesis 12: 1-3

Since much of what we shall say about the triple theme of election, covenant, and mission is closely related to the Call of Abraham in Genesis 12: 1-3, a key-passage in the interpretation of biblical history and theology, and therefore in our Hebrew-Christian heritage, we shall quote it here in full:

"Now the LORD said to Abram, Go from your country and your kindred and your father's house to the land that I will show you. And I will make of you a great nation, and I will bless you, and make your name great, so that you will be a blessing. I will bless those who bless you, and him who curses you I will curse; and by you all the families of the earth will bless themselves."

The alternate translation of the last clause in the RSV footnote should also be noted, since it will come in for considerable mention in the course of our interpretation of the passage as a whole: "in you all the families of the earth will be blessed."

It should also be noted from the beginning that variations of this line are found in four other places in Genesis: 18: 18; 22: 17, 18; 26: 4; and 28: 13, 14 (all a part of the story of Abraham).

Equally significant is the fact that it is found twice in the New Testament: in Acts 3: 25, 26, as the conclusion to Peter's sermon in the temple, which brought about the conversion of almost five thousand men; and in Galatians 3: 8, where Paul says that it was a preaching of the gospel beforehand to Abraham. See the whole chapter for perspective.

We shall analyze the Call of Abraham carefully; but before we do so, we must look at a few definitions of terms. What do we mean when we speak of election, covenant, and mission? One book which helps us much at this point is Edmond Jacob's *Theology of the Old Testament*.

Definitions

What is *election*, in the sense in which we use it in this chapter? Edmond Jacob defines it in this way "Every intervention by God in history is an election; either when he chooses a place in which to make more especial manifestation of his presence, or when he chooses a people to carry out his intentions, or when he chooses a man to be his representative or his messenger, the Old Testament God is the one who has universal sovereignty at his disposal, and shows it by the free use that he makes of it." (*Theology of the Old Testament,* p. 201).

The technical term for it in Hebrew is the verb *bachar,* which means *to choose*: a free unmotivated choice, among several possibilities. Other verbs bring out the aspect of the call, of belonging, of separation, of setting apart, of interest and concern for. Implicitly it suggests a special relationship for a special purpose. The idea may be present without the specific verb mentioned above. The theological implications of election are always those of a completely autonomous divine authority which acts by selecting someone or something for a purpose determined by God.

A few of the more significant illustrations of election in the sense in which we understand it here may help us to understand the concept. Let us mention six:

The call of Abraham, of which we shall have much to say in this chapter. Genesis 12: 1-3. Isaiah 29: 22.

The redemption of Israel out of slavery, of which we shall say much in the next chapter. Exodus 1-18.

The burning bush, selected as the place where Moses received his call. Exodus 3: 1ff.

The divinely selected place of worship within Israel, with symbolic significance for worship everywhere and always. Exodus 20: 4.

Christian discipleship. John 15: 16 (among many New Testament passages).

Christian baptism, conversion, ministry, within the Christian Church.

Closely related to election is covenant. What is meant by *covenant?* The full meaning of the term as we use it here transcends a definition. See Milton, *God's Covenant of Blessing.* But an attempt at a definition must be made. Karl Barth sees a connection between covenant and creation. "The covenant is the goal of creation, creation is the way to the covenant." Insofar as covenant is equivalent to *relationship* this is true. We have seen that the concept of relationship was inherent in man's creation in the image of God. But this has nothing to do with the covenant in its redemptive aspect; and it is in that sense that we want to think and speak of it now.

48

One of the commonest definitions is in terms of the German word Zusammengehörigkeit, or "a relationship of belonging between two parties." This will do if we bear in mind that the covenant is always unilateral in origin; it is *God's covenant with man.* As such it may consist of divine promises or of commandments, or of both. When man responds to it in faith or in obedience, or in both, it becomes a mutual relationship. As far as Fallen Man is concerned covenant is closely linked with election. Edmond Jacob says that election is *"the initial act* by which Yahweh comes into relation with his people *and the permanent reality* which assures the constancy of that bond." This permanent reality is the covenant.

There are references to several covenants in the Old Testament, all essentially one in relationship and purpose, and leading up to the fulfillment in the new covenant in the blood of Christ. For the sake of illustration we list a few of the covenants mentioned.

The key to the whole redemptive covenant concept is the covenant of blessing with Abraham. The analysis of Genesis 12: 1-3 will show why this covenant is so important.

The covenant with Abraham includes, or finds part of its fulfillment, in the covenant with Israel as a people. The most important section for study here is Exodus 19-24, which relates first of all to the Exodus redemption which leads up to it and then to the concept of Torah or divine instruction in the right way as an integral part of it.

God's covenant with David, which was the basis for the kingship in Israel, has a significant place in both the history and prophecy of Israel. It is also the theme of psalmody as in Psalm 89. We shall return to it frequently as we look into the triple concept of history, prophecy, and psalmody in the Old Testament.

One of the great prophetic passages in the Old Testament is Jeremiah 31: 31-34, which announces the terms of "the new covenant" that God promises to make because his people have broken the first. In a sense it reiterates the terms of the original covenant with Abraham and with his descendants, the people of Israel; at the same time it anticipates the terms of "the new covenant" in the New Testament, which is the fulfillment of the whole covenant concept as it relates to our Hebrew-Christian heritage.

There is still a third term that needs definition. What is meant by *mission*?

Again we turn to Edmond Jacob's *Theology of the Old Testament:* "The election of Israel was to lead of necessity to a missionary duty."

That is, there can be no divine election, nor covenant, without mission. God's election or covenant is never for the purpose of a selfish spiritual privilege or blessing. We are blessed for a purpose. We shall see this clearly in our analysis of the Call of Abraham, with its forward look to the Covenant with Israel and to the people of God in the New Testament Church. It is a fundamental principle of our Hebrew-Christian heritage that election, covenant, and mission, in that order, are inseparable.

THE STORY OF ABRAHAM

We shall turn now to an analysis of the great scriptural passage in Genesis 12: 1-3. In my judgment it is the key to an understanding of the whole Bible, from Genesis to the end of the New Testament. We may refer to it as the Call of Abraham, or as God's promise to Abraham, or as the beginning of the Covenant of Blessing: in any case it involves the triple concept of election, covenant, and mission. We shall attempt a five-point analysis and interpretation.

What do we note in the experience of Abraham here, and as amplified elsewhere? We note:

First, That he was confronted with a significant Choice. This choice had two sides to it.

God, the LORD, Yahweh, *chose Abraham* for an as yet undefined purpose. Here is the mysterious reality of election, or of particularism, on the part of God. See von Rad's *GENESIS*, p. 150; Claude Tresmontant's *A Study of Hebrew Thought*, p. 64. In the Genesis story the choice took the form of *a Command*: "Go;" which in a deeper sense constituted a Call to Obedience. See Gen. 12: 1.

Abraham's choice was whether he should obey or disobey. Obedience is the big word in Abraham's life. So also is faith; for you simply cannot separate obedience from a preceding or accompanying faith. Abraham obeyed God because he believed in the LORD. See Genesis 12: 4; 15: 6; and 22: 15-18. According to Romans 4 and Galatians 3 Abraham is the supreme Old Testament example of a man of obedient faith. His response to God's command was given in the obedience of faith.

But more is involved in the Choice than a mere change of geographical location: see Genesis 12: 1. Learn to read between the lines! Learn to read the Old Testament in the perspective of history, both biblical and secular. Remember Abraham's home background in Ur of the Chaldeans, and later in Haran. Leonard Woolley's excavations at Ur have revealed a culture saturated with polytheism, with "Moon-god worship" as its chief feature. Something of the same can be said about Haran. The signficant thing is that of such "Moon-god" worship there is no trace in the Abraham story in Genesis. Occasional lapses into idolatry there were among his descendants; but Abraham's own life is singularly free from any form of worship other than that of *the living God.* How shall we account for it? There may be a hint at the answer in Isaiah 29: 22, where we read of "the LORD who redeemed Abraham." Redemption is one form of election. Abraham was redeemed from the syncretistic and polytheistic religion of heathendom, in order to become the representative of a new form of worship and a new way of life. The Choice of which we have been speaking therefore involved for Abraham *a new Way of Life,* with a new knowledge of God as the living God, and with a closer walk with this God which made him known as "the friend of God:" see Isaiah 41: 8; II Chronicles 20: 7; and James 2: 23. It was an experience comparable to the one described in I Peter 1: 18-19, "a ransom from the futile ways inherited from your fathers." From every point of view it was a significant Choice indeed: both God's choice or election of Abraham, and Abraham's choice of the new Way shown him by God.

For in the experience of Abraham we note next:

Second, That the right Choice was Encouraged by a great promise: "I will bless you." Unlike the Choice, which in a sense was mutual, this is a pure promise, a promised act of God in the continuing future, an act of grace: in fact, *a Covenant.*

How shall we understand this promise of blessing? In the context in which it stands it may suggest some material blessings: for example, 1) prosperity (land), (vs. 7; 2) progeny (a great nation, a numerous seed), vs. 2 (see also 22: 15-18); fame (a great name), vs. 2. But if we were to limit the promise of blessing to these material things, it would be a case of wishful thinking in the light of what follows in the Old Testament. There is a spiritual quality to this blessing at which we have already hinted. The highest blessing that a man can experience is the very presence of God, the true knowledge of God, the walk before God (see Genesis 48: 15, the sense of friendship with God, the "your God — my people" relationship of the Covenant (see Genesis 17: 7-8). This religious interpretation is supported by the rest of the Abraham story (see Genesis 15: 1, 6 and 22: 1-19), by the rest of the Old Testament (as we shall see when we study the history of God's people Israel and his covenant with them), and by the New Testament (see especially Galatians 3). It will receive support from what comes next in our analysis of Genesis 12: 1-3. According to our Hebrew-Christian heritage Abraham was the prototype of what men of faith and obedience ought to be.

For in the experience of Abraham we note next:

Third, That he was given a unique Charge or Commission: to be a blessing. At least, I personally cannot understand the last clause of verse 2 in any other way; and I think that it expresses correctly the teaching of our Hebrew-Christian heritage. The Hebrew verb in this clause is in the imperative. ASV translates quite literally, "and be thou a blessing." RSV translates as "an intended result" clause, "so that you will be a blessing." This is technically permissible as far as the Hebrew imperative is concerned, and there is really no contradiction between the two versions; although RSV tends to obscure ever so slightly *Abraham's active participation* in this matter of being a blessing. It is, from God's point of view, a command or a commission rather than a promise; and Abraham has really nothing to say about it except to decide whether he is willing to accept the commission.

Perhaps we should not so quickly have ruled out the element of promise in what seems to be an outright command; for the question inevitably arises, How can anyone become or be a blessing? It certainly does not come naturally, as if we could just determine by ourselves that this is what we shall be. We must first receive a blessing from God, a spiritual gift that we can share with others. That is why the sequence of thought in this passage is so very significant: first, the promise by God, "I will bless you," and then the command empowered by the promise, "and be a blessing." We share what we have received and experienced of the blessings of God. It was so with Abraham. It is so with us. There is no other way for any man to be a blessing to others than by first receiving "every spiritual blessing" from God. And yet, the wording reminds us that this giving or sharing is not as though we were handing over something apart from us, quite impersonally: what we are talking about here is *something lived,* a blessing of God which has become a part of us, so that in faith and obedience we are actually enabled to become or to be a blessing by our very lives. The verb is in the active: *"be* a blessing." Structurally this Commission is at the heart of the passage that narrates the Call of Abraham, as it is also of our Hebrew-Christian heritage. Election, covenant, and mission: these three combine to form the essence of God's purpose with Abraham, and with us.

But there is more to the paragraph before us; for in the experience of Abraham we note next:

Fourth, That the attitude of others towards him would be the Criterion for God's judgment of blessing or curse upon them: "I will bless those who bless you, and him who curses you I will curse."

Admittedly this is a difficult saying! Therefore it is usually passed over lightly by the reader, and even by the exegete. But the words are there, and we have no right to evade them. If we think only of an attitude towards a man, or towards a people descended from him, they don't make sense. They do make sense if we think of an attitude towards that for which Abraham stood: his religion, his God, his faith, his way of life as a walk before the living God (Genesis 48: 15). We must look at the words in a much deeper, in a far larger, perspective than simply as a statement of the reaction of others to Abraham as a man or to Israel as a nation. The apostle Paul helps us to interpret the whole passage, including these words, in Galatians 3; where we see Abraham as the prototype of all men who have faith, a faith resting on the acts and promises of God. To bless him is therefore to share his faith, and that brings blessing to him who does so; to curse Abraham is to reject his faith, his God, and his way of life, and that can only bring a curse instead of a blessing in return. So central and so significant is the Abraham experience in our Hebrew-Christian heritage. The significance will become clearer as we see how the experience of Abraham is related to that of the people of Israel, and later to that of the Christian Church.

And so we come to the last point in our analysis of Abraham's Call to be a Blessing. We note:

Fifth, The Climactic Declaration of purpose in verse 3b: "and by you all the families of the earth will bless themselves." Or, as we read in the RSV footnote, "in you all the families of the earth will be blessed." We shall discuss the difference in translation shortly. In a sense this is a recapitulation of the Commission to be a blessing, worded now as a promise instead of a command. That is why the whole passage is sometimes called the Promise to Abraham. In Galatians 3: 8 Paul calls it *the gospel* preached beforehand to Abraham. Peter, in Acts 3: 25, calls it simply *the covenant,* which now found final fulfillment in God's servant Jesus. God sent his servant, first to the people of Israel, Abraham's posterity, and then to the whole Gentile world, for the purpose of "turning every one of you from your wickedness." This spiritual interpretation of the mission of the servant is a significant confirmation of what we have been saying

53

about Genesis 12: 1-3. It is in fulfillment of the promise to Abraham that God "has blessed us in Christ with every spiritual blessing in the heavenly places" (see Ephesians 1: 3 and context).

We turn back to the Genesis story itself to note the importance of this promise for Old Testament history and theology. It is found five times, with slight but significant variations in wording, in what we call *patriarchal history*. The first is of course in connection with Abraham's Call in Genesis 12: 1-3. The second is in Genesis 18: 17-18, where it furnishes the motivation for God's taking Abraham into his confidence and permitting him to intercede for Sodom, and for Lot. The third, and perhaps the most remarkable instance, is in Genesis 22: 15-18, after God's testing of Abraham on Mount Moriah: here the obedience of Abraham is commended, and the promise is renewed not only to him but to his descendants. The fourth is in Genesis 26: 3-5, where it is reaffirmed to Isaac after Abraham's death. The fifth is in Genesis 28: 13-14, when it was renewed to Jacob at Bethel: in the vision of the ladder set up on earth and reaching to heaven, with the angels of God ascending and descending on it.

We promised that we would say something about the linguistic problem of translation. Which translation of the Hebrew verb is to be preferred, the passive (as in ASV) or the reflective (as in RSV)? In the five instances cited in Genesis there are two verbal forms used: one which is invariably reflective and the other more commonly used as a passive. See Milton, *God's Covenant of Blessing*, pp. 52-54. Older versions, such as the Septuagint, translated the verb in all five Genesis passages as a passive; and this is reflected in the form of the New Testament quotations. More recent versions have leaned towards a reflective translation throughout, except in the New Testament. Why, we may ask, must it be translated the same everywhere despite the differences in the verbal form? Why not recognize that the biblical authors intended to give two different emphases: one, on Abraham as *the medium* of God's blessing, and two, *on the desire of others to share* that blessing? Both emphases are biblically and theologically correct. Both belong to a right understanding of the promise to Abraham in our Hebrew-Christian heritage. The Swedish version of 1917 correctly makes this distinction. So also does so eminent a theologian as Otto Procksch in his *Theology of the Old Testament* (German edition). The RSV footnotes enable us to see where the passive translation is permissible if not to be preferred. In either translation we see Abraham as a blessing, a mediator of God's blessing to the world.

54

The election to be a blessing concerns not only Abraham but his seed, or his descendants, as we see from the Genesis passages; especially Genesis 22: 15-18. The Hebrew noun *zera* is a singular-collective noun. It can therefore refer to an individual or to a group. In the Old Testament we may refer it to Isaac as the son of promise and also to his descendants as the chosen people. In the New Testament Paul applies it first in the singular to Christ (Galatians 3: 16) and then in the plural to all who are Christ's, because they are men of faith (Galatians 3: 29). Whether singular or plural, we have the same combination of election and mission, the call to receive and to be a blessing.

It should be noted, of course, how closely *land* and *nation* are coupled with *blessing* in Genesis, and in the Old Testament generally; but not so in the New Testament. Even in Genesis the blessing is always in the climactic spot. The others were simply means to an end. Abraham and through him Israel were called to be a blessing to the peoples of the earth in a unique spiritual sense. Therefore the problem of election vanishes. It does not imply favoritism on the part of God. It implies rather a call to servanthood. The promise of divine blessing to Abraham is inseparable from his Commission to be a blessing. In this connection we suggest a careful reading of the remarkable prophecy in Isaiah 19: 24-25, where Assyria and Egypt, ancient enemies of Israel, are included with Israel as recipients of the blessing of the LORD of hosts and also in the commission to be a blessing in the midst of the earth. This is one of the great missionary passages in the Old Testament; it is void of all meaning if separated from the spiritual interpretation which we have tried to give to the Call of Abraham to be the spiritual father of all men who share his faith. This is not to say that God fulfilled his purpose of election, covenant, and mission in Abraham; but he certainly *began* to reveal that purpose through him; the concept of election-covenant-mission for the first time assumed the proportions of a major motif in our Hebrew-Christian heritage.

A Summary

Finally, by way of summary of the significance of Genesis 12:1-3 and of the Call of Abraham and of the triple concept of election, covenant, and mission for our Hebrew-Christian heritage, we add a few quotations.

From Wilhelm Möller, an older, less wellknown, fundamentalist writer: "In Genesis we encounter the beginning of the history of salvation — and the prehistory of the Israelitish people. The first eleven chapters show that all mankind can be saved, that it needs to be saved, and that God has begun to carry into effect his work of salvation. At the point where the history of humanity becomes the family history of the patriarchs, there stands as an entrance inscription which cannot be misunderstood God's promise to Abraham in 12: 3, 'In you all the families of the earth will be blessed.' The promise in Genesis goes before the law which is given in the remaining books of Moses. Accordingly we meet already here the line of thought which Paul later has so sharply chiseled out, especially in Galatians 3."

From Gerhard von Rad, a modern scholar, thoroughly acquainted with the methods of Form Criticism: "The transition from primeval history to sacred history occurs abruptly and surprisingly in vs. 1-3. All at once and precipitously the universal field of vision narrows; world and humanity, the entire ecumenical fullness, are submerged, and all interest is concentrated upon a single man. Previously the narrative concerned humanity as a whole, man's creation and essential character, woman, sin, suffering, humanity, nations, all of them universal themes. In vs. 1, as though after a break, the particularism of election begins, and with it the 'scandal.' From the multitude of nations God chooses a man, looses him from his tribal ties, and makes him the beginner of a new nation and the recipient of great promises of salvation. What is promised to Abraham reaches far beyond Israel; indeed, it has universal meaning for all generations on earth. Thus that difficult question about God's relationship to the nations is answered, and precisely where one least expects it. At the beginning of the way into an emphatically exclusive covenant-relation there is already a word about the end of this way, namely, an allusion to a final, universal unchaining of the salvation promised to Abraham. Truly flesh and blood did not inspire this view beyond Israel and its saving relation to God!" *(Commentary on Genesis,* p. 150).

It is remarkable how close *fundamentalism* (Möller) is to *Form Criticism* (von Rad) in its theological interpretation here!

Many other writers hold the same high view of the significance of Genesis 12: 1-3 and the Call of Abraham in biblical history and theology. We cite three briefly.

From Charles T. Fritsch, Princeton professor of Old Testament, in *The Layman's Bible Commentary*: "According to Genesis 12: 1-3 God calls one man out from among the multitude of nations to be the channel of his saving grace to the world — to be a blessing to 'all the families of the earth.' God has not forgotten mankind. — This is the saving link, as it were, between the wide-scale history of Genesis 1-11 and the 'holy history' of Genesis 12 to the end of the Bible. God's redemptive purpose for the world now becomes focused on a specific person."

From Herbert C. Alleman, Lutheran theologian, in *Alleman-Flack's Old Testament Commentary*: "The steps by which Abram passed from moon-god worship to the worship of the spiritual God of Israel are not preserved for us in Genesis. — The point of the Genesis story is that without the divine call Abram would not have made the transition. — Abram was the first man to go out from an old and cultured civilization in the interest of his religion. He went out to find the true God because God was calling him. He was the first pilgrim of faith, the father of all those who obey the divine voice. In thee shall all the families of the earth be blessed (cf. 18: 18 and 28: 14) through the revelation given to Israel and fulfilled in Christianity."

From Bruce Vawter, a Catholic scholar, in *Paths through Genesis*: "Through God's mercy Abraham is removed from the idolatry and pagan error in which he had been reared and directed towards the land of Palestine which would become the inheritance of his descendants. From Abraham would spring the nation of God's choice, and from that nation would come forth Christ the Savior. The purpose of God's blessing of Abraham is thus the measure of its greatness: 'In you shall all the nations of the earth be blessed.' "

My own conclusion is this: Genesis 12: 1-3 is the Prelude to a majestic sacred drama in Two Acts, enacted in history; the first Act being the history of Israel as the Covenant People of God, chosen for the purpose of being a spiritual blessing to the nations; and the second Act being the Call to discipleship within the Christian Church, which involves the proclamation of the Gospel. Throughout the drama we see the three concepts so significant to our Hebrew-Christian heritage: election, covenant, and mission. See Milton, *God's Covenant of Blessing*, for a fuller treatment.

Chapter 5

THE CONCEPT OF REDEMPTION

We have said, and we repeat, that in the discussion of any significant concept in our Hebrew-Christian heritage there will necessarily be some repetition and review.

We saw this overlapping of biblical concepts in our first three chapters, where we spoke of God, Creation, and Man. We shall see it in this chapter where our discussion will center around the concept of Redemption. According to Isaiah 29: 22 the LORD redeemed Abraham. In fact, redemption is actually equivalent to election as an intervention of God in history. When God called Abraham to a new manner of life based on a new knowledge of God and faith in him as the One and only living God it was both an act of election and an act of redemption. We have noted that the Call of Abraham included not only him and his immediate family but his descendants through Isaac, the people of Israel. Everything that is said of Abraham, especially his Commission to be a blessing, applies also to Israel as the chosen people of God. In fact 'Blessed to be a Blessing,' with Abraham as its first and chief illustration, is the Introduction to the two-act historical drama or religious consummation which comprises the rest of the Bible: the history and mission of God's people Israel, and the life and ministry of Christ and his Church.

It is primarily in the history of Israel that the Redemption motif in the Old Testament is to be seen. We call it usually the Exodus-redemption, meaning the deliverance of Israel out of slavery in Egypt. The story of this redemption is found in Exodus 1-18. The key-passage to its interpretation is Exodus 19: 3-6, which we shall both quote and analyze later on in the chapter; and thinking of our Hebrew-Christian heritage a good theme for what we shall have to say is "Redeemed to be a Responsible People of God," or as we might put it, "Redeemed to be a Blessing."

Introduction

There are a few things that might be said by way of Introduction before we consider the Exodus passage.

In *The Book of the Acts of God* G. Ernest Wright refers to five great historical events which he calls "faith-events," because the biblical writers interpreted them as "saving acts of God." The five events are: 1) the call of the fathers (beginning with Abraham); 2) the deliverance of Israel from bondage in Egypt (or the Exodus); 3) the Sinai covenant (including the giving of the Torah or the Law); 4) the conquest of Canaan as in inheritance from God, the land of promise; and 5) the covenant with David (including his conquests and government), with its Messianic overtones. As Wright says, "When an Israelite confessed his faith, he simply gave an interpreted version of his national tradition." Since these five events mentioned by Wright are all interrelated they might be said to be equally important; but the exodus from Egypt, interpreted as "God's freeing of a people from slavery," does seem to have a unique or central place in Israel's faith as well as theology. We have already seen the significance of the Call of Abraham in our Hebrew-Christian heritage. We shall now consider the significance of the Exodus-redemption, which is a step in the fulfillment of the Covenant of Blessing with Abraham.

There are many significant Old Testament references to the redemption of Israel from Egypt, of which we shall name a few here at the outset. They are selected because of the significance of the context, and because they therefore serve to illustrate vividly the extent to which the Exodus-redemption constituted a genuine "faith-event" in the religion of Israel.

1. There is first the preamble to the Ten Commandments in Exodus 20: 4 and Deuteronomy 5: 6. "I am the LORD your God, who brought you out of the land of Egypt, out of the house of bondage." The prelude to the commandments is a redeeming act of God. To read the commandments without attention to the prelude is to interpret them out of their historical perspective. It would be perfectly proper to insert before the commandments the little word "therefore," as Paul does in Romans 12: 1. "I appeal to you therefore, brethren, by the mercies of God" is the plea in both Exodus and Romans, in both the Old Testament and the New. It is only when God by an act of redemption in grace and mercy has created for himself a people of God that the commandments become what they are intended to be, a guide in the good and in the right way (see I Samuel 12: 23).

2. Then there is the great covenant passage in Deuteronomy 7: 6-8, to which we shall return later. We quote it here: "For you are a people

59

holy to the LORD your God; the LORD your God has chosen you to be a people for his own possession, out of all the peoples that are on the face of the earth. It was not because you were more in number than any other people that the LORD set his love upon you and chose you, for you were the fewest of all peoples; but it is because the LORD loves you, and is keeping the oath which he swore to your fathers, that the LORD has brought you out with a mighty hand, and redeemed you from the house of bondage, from the hand of Pharaoh king of Egypt." We observe the same concept of election as in the Call of Abraham, with which this passage is so closely linked. God *chose* Israel to be his people for two reasons: because of his free, sovereign love, and because of his faithfulness to the promise given to Abraham and the fathers. The paragraph says that God "chose you" and also that he "redeemed you," which mean essentially the same thing. That is, "God redeemed you" is essentially equivalent to "God elected you;" with this difference that the word *redeemed* brings out more clearly the act of God in history which is involved in Israel's election. The redemption of Israel out of slavery in Egypt was a high point in Israel's faith and worship. It also sheds important illumination on the spiritual teaching in our Hebrew-Christian heritage concerning God as the Redeemer.

3. There is also the "number one" item in the reminder-list of "the saving acts of the LORD" in Micah 6: 4-5. "For I brought you up from the land of Egypt, and redeemed you from the house of bondage." The whole list is significant in terms of Israel's historical experience and religious faith, but it begins with an act of redemption. We find the same sequence in Amos 2: 10-11. It reflects the prophetic point of view of Israel's heritage, which is also a part of ours.

4. Then there is the poignant statement in Hosea 11: 1, "When Israel was a child, I loved him, and out of Egypt I called my son." The verse should be read in the perspective of the whole chapter, or at least of verses 1-4. There is the tender comparison with a father teaching his son to walk; and the painful experience of having his child so often turn away from him in search of other gods. Yet the love of God for his people remains true, even when he must discipline them for their good. One of the most wonderful passages in the Old Testament is found in Hosea 11: 8-9, and while its first application is to Israel it has a bearing on the concept of redemption as a whole.

"How can I give you up, O Ephraim!
    How can I hand you over, O Israel!
How can I make you like Admah!
    How can I treat you like Zeboiim!
My heart recoils within me,
    my compassion grows warm and tender.
I will not execute my fierce anger,
    I will not again destroy Ephraim;
for I am God and not man,
    the Holy One in your midst,
    and I will not come to destroy."

The prophet Hosea, at least, had caught a vision of the living God as being also a loving God, a faithful Savior, a Redeemer; and his insight began with his correct understanding of the Exodus-redemption as an act of God.

5. Then there is also the great prophetic passage in Isaiah 63: 7-14, a retrospect recounting "the steadfast love of the LORD" and his "great goodness to the house of Israel." The prophecy includes these lines:

"in his love and in his pity he redeemed them;
he lifted them up and carried them all the days of old."

The whole paragraph deserves careful reading. It will be obvious to the reader that the prophet is speaking against the background of the exodus, the wilderness journey, and finally the conquest of and rest in the land of promise. In one sense the exodus redemption covers all of these events but in its more specific sense it refers to the deliverance out of the slavery in Egypt.

6. We have by no means exhausted the list of significant references to the exodus as "a faith-event" in the Old Testament; but we should keep in mind that we are not limited to direct verbal allusions to the exodus as an act of redemption. What is more significant is the fact that the Exodus-event, seen in its broadest sense as including everything from the initial act of deliverance from slavery in Egypt to the inheritance of the promised land, undergirds all Old Testament history, prophecy, psalmody, worship, as well as the faith and life of Israel as a Responsible People of God. For this you must take my word, of course, until you have time to read and see for yourself. It is a statement, however, that can be verified. Reading Eric Wahlstrom's book, *God Who Redeems,* would help you to see the redemptive activity of God in a somewhat broader perspective than that of the single experience that we call the Exodus-redemption. We shall try to do the same thing before we conclude this study of redemption in our Hebrew-Christian heritage. In a postscript to this chapter we shall

refer to a book by Gustaf Wingren of Lund, *An Exodus Theology*. We mention it here because the very title is suggestive. We simply cannot escape the significance of the "exodus" in relation to the faith of Israel; and it is not stretching the point to say of this act of God by which he chose Israel to be his people what Gerhard von Rad said of the Call of Abraham and of the promise to him in Genesis 12: 1-3, "What is promised to Abraham reaches far beyond Israel; indeed, it has universal meaning for all generations on earth." What we are searching for is a significance which makes it truly a part of our Hebrew-Christian heritage, with emphasis upon its meaning for Christianity.

The History of the Exodus

The historical record of the redemption of Israel out of Egypt is found in Exodus 1-18. The section makes interesting reading, and it is worth reading in its entirety; but we are interested in it now chiefly as background for an intensive analysis of the key-passage in Exodus 19: 1-6. Let us therefore simply call attention to some selected passages which will serve both as illustration and as outline.

It is from the Joseph story in Genesis 37-50 that we learn how it came about that the family of Israel was in Egypt at all, and at first as honored guests.

In Exodus 1: 1-7 we learn that the 70 persons who came down to Egypt multiplied greatly; and from 1: 8ff. we learn of a change in fortune whereby instead of being honored guests they became a persecuted and afflicted people. It is not our purpose in this book to delve into the reasons for the change, though from non-biblical sources we know or can guess quite accurately what those reasons were. The bible story is chiefly concerned with the raising up of a man who should lead his people out of their bondage and affliction. That man was Moses. After telling about his birth and training we come at last to his Call to serve, in Exodus 3, at the burning bush. The theophany is significant, but the terms of his call even more so. We quote from Exodus 3: 7-10: "Then the LORD said, 'I have seen the affliction of my people who are in Egypt, and have heard their cry because of their taskmasters; I know their sufferings, and I have come down to deliver them out of the hand of the Egyptians, and to bring them up out of that land to a good and broad land flowing with milk and honey —. And now, behold, the cry of the people of Israel has come to me, and I have seen the oppression with which the Egyptians oppress them.

Come, I will send you to Pharaoh that you may bring forth my people, the sons of Israel, out of Egypt.' "

Note the significant words "affliction," "sufferings," and "oppression" as descriptive of Israel's condition. Note the promise of the LORD, "I have come down to deliver them." Note the Commission given to Moses in verse 10. The deliverance would be an act of God, but in it he would make use of his servant Moses.

We pass over Moses' excuses and God's answers, interesting and significant as they are, to note in Exodus 5: 1 for the first time the words addressed to Pharaoh, "Let my people go." The demand is repeated again and again, until at last Pharaoh yields.

But before this we have one of the more significant passages in this history of the exodus. RSV gives it the heading "The Promises of God," and it is found in Exodus 6: 2-8. Once more the whole passage is worth reading; but we shall quote only verses 6-7: "Say therefore to the people of Israel, 'I am the LORD, and I will bring you out from under the burdens of the Egyptians, and I will deliver you from their bondage, and I will *redeem* you with an outstretched arm and with great acts of judgment, and I will take you for my people, and I will be your God; and you shall know that I am the LORD your God, who has brought you out from under the burdens of the Egyptians.' " The focus is clearly on a redemptive act of God, and the promise of coming redemption is meant to inspire faith. As we see from verse 9, faith was slow in coming; but even this did not hinder the redemptive purpose of God. In due time faith did recognize the redemptive activity of God, and Israel acknowledged God not only as the Creator but as a Redeemer; and with this acknowledgment came an ever deepening insight into the ultimate nature of redemption as a spiritual experience, a deliverance from all manner of evil, whether it affect the body or the soul. There is more than a superficial connection between the exodus concept of redemption and the New Testament concept of an eternal redemption through Jesus Christ. Keep the thought in mind. We shall have more to say about it later.

We are still studying the history of the exodus, however. Finally, in Exodus 12, on the night of the first Passover, the promised redemption and release became a reality. After four hundred and thirty years they were free at last. In Exodus 12: 42 we read: "It was a night of watching by the LORD, to bring them out of the land of Egypt; so this same night is a night of watching kept to the LORD by all the people of Israel throughout their generations." The chapter concludes with this terse historical statement: "And on that very day the LORD brought the people of Israel out of the land of Egypt by their hosts."

One thing more needs to be said before we leave the historical record to turn our attention to the great theological key-passage in Exodus 19: 1-6. The redemptive theme continues through the Red Sea episode, and from there in all the events from the crossing of the Red Sea to the arrival at Sinai. The terminology of redemption is not used, but the experience of the redemptive acts of God is ever present. Israel was delivered from their slavery in Egypt. Israel was on the way to the promised land. What is more important, Israel was on the way to a significant meeting with the LORD their Redeemer as a prelude to the renewal of Covenant with them at Sinai. It is to that meeting, which is keynoted for us in Exodus 19: 1-6, that we turn our attention next.

Exodus 19: 1-6

Redeemed to be a Responsible People of God

This is one of the great passages in the Old Testament. It is also the spiritual interpretation of the history of the exodus and its purpose. Its theme, as we shall see, is "Redeemed to be a Responsible People of God." There are spiritual overtones to it which look forward to the New Testament, where in I Peter 2: 9-10 much of its wording is applied by the apostle to the New Testament Church. The Exodus-redemption is a type of, or a preparatory step for, that greater act of redemption which we call the eternal redemption through the blood of Christ.

It is worth quoting in full: "And Moses went up to God, and the LORD called him out of the mountain, saying, 'Thus you shall say to the house of Jacob, and tell the people of Israel: You have seen what I did to the Egyptians, and how I bore you on eagles' wings and brought you to myself. Now therefore, if you will obey my voice and keep my covenant, you shall be my own possession among all people; for all the earth in mine, and you shall be to me a kingdom of priests and a holy nation. These are the words which you shall speak to the children of Israel.' "

1. Let us make five general preliminary observations about this passage before we look more closely at its message.

First, Seen in its proper perspective in the historical narrative, the time and place is when Israel first arrived at Mount Sinai, the mount of the Law.

Second, Seen in its literary context, it looks both backward and forward; it is at the same time a resumé and a prelude, it refers both to redemption and to covenant.

Third, Viewed in theological perspective, it is presented as a prophetic word of God through Moses which interprets events past, present, and future, as acts of God.

Fourth, Seen as covenant theology, it is not only the Introduction to the formal making of a covenant between God and Israel (see Exodus 24) but also a clear summary of the fundamental principles of the covenant from Abraham on (see Genesis 12: 1-3).

Fifth, Seen in the light of the intertestamental relationship the spirit and much of the letter of this Exodus passage is reflected in the New Testament. We have seen that to be true of I Peter 2: 9-10, but it is true elsewhere also.

2. As we begin to examine the passage itself we confront a fundamental question: In what direction does the action move, that is, the action of the spoken word?

It moves from God to Moses (the LORD called him) and through Moses to the people (say, tell the people of Israel). The initiative in the action of the word is from the LORD. It is his word. The same is true, as we shall see, of the covenant: he initiates it and calls it "my covenant." The same is true of redemption, the theme which we are now pursuing. It is an act of God. The first person singular pronoun, representing God, fairly leaps to meet the eye: it occurs eight times in three verses. So does the pronoun *you*, which occurs six times. God's word, his act of redemption and his covenant, are all addressed to Israel: Israel is involved in God's redemptive purpose and in the previous historical experience.

3. For note in verse four the clear, beautiful statement of the act of redemption by which God had brought Israel to this holy encounter at Sinai, and to the giving of the Torah (see chapter 6), and to the making of the covenant a mutual relationship of "belonging together." In a sense it is a resumé of Exodus 1-18 with its redemption motif which we have already examined.

"You have seen what I did:" that is, you have experienced the acts of God in your behalf. They did not need to go by hearsay. They were eye-witnesses of those historical events now interpreted as a revelation of God's redeeming power and grace.

65

You have seen what I did to the Egyptians; that is, you have seen my great judgments against the oppressor for the deliverance of my people Israel. Elsewhere in the Old Testament they are sometimes called his righteous acts, and also his saving acts. The religious truth which it illustrates is this, that judgment is always the obverse side of redemption or salvation. When God redeems men it is from some evil, some affliction, some oppression, whether it be material or spiritual or both; and in order to accomplish his redemption he works through mighty acts of judgment on the evil that afflicts us. This was true in the Old Testament of the Exodus-redemption. It is true in the New Testament of the eternal redemption through the blood of Christ from sin, death, and the power of the devil. It is a fundamental truth in our Hebrew-Christian heritage.

You have seen how I bore you on eagles' wings. This refers to the positive side of redemption. They were eye-witnesses of God's saving grace, both in the initial experience of the exodus deliverance and in the subsequent experience on the way. The language is beautiful and symbolic, suggesting strength and security in a physical as well as in a spiritual sense. See Isaiah 63: 9 and context.

You have seen how I brought you to myself. This denotes God's gracious Presence. They had been brought into his fellowship, love, protection, and care. The reference is to the "your God — my people" relationship. That experience had already begun. It began in the darkness of the Passover night when the light of God's favor shone upon them in their dwellings. It continued all the way from the Red Sea and the wilderness wanderings to Sinai. It was to reach its climax in the Sinai experience: in the giving of the Torah and in the making of the Covenant. To interpret these words as meaning only their historical arrival at Sinai is to minimize the deep spiritual significance that lay in the exodus-redemption. God brought them to himself in a far deeper sense than that. The exodus-redemption was a spiritual experience. God brought Israel to himself in a new spiritual relationship. The nature of that relationship we shall explore, for it belongs to our Hebrew-Christian heritage.

4. And so we note the statement of purpose in verse 5: you shall be my own possession among all peoples. The Hebrew word used here is a rare and richly meaningful one, my *segullah*. Various translations have been given to this word, and each sheds some light on its actual meaning. The Hebrew lexicon, edited by Brown, Driver, and Briggs, renders it as "valued property, peculiar treasure." The American Jewish Version of the Old Testament translates it as "mine own treasure." A later Jewish trans-

lation, the Torah of 1962, renders it as "my treasured possession." We have noticed the RSV rendering as "my own possession." Personally I like the translation in Smith-Goodspeed's *An American Translation:* "my very own." It is quite obvious that there are two facets to the word *segullah:* ownership and value. It is closely related to the concept of the covenant as "a mutual belonging together." Israel belonged to God as his people. God regarded Israel as his people as his peculiar treasure, as his very own. The same is true of "the people of God" concept in the New Testament. It is a part of the wonders of our Hebrew-Christian heritage.

5. Redeemed, or elected, to be in a special sense a people of God; so far we have come in our study of Exodus 19: 3-6 and of the theme based on it, "Redeemed to be a Responsible People of God." But now we come to the key-word in our theme: "Responsible." God has acted first; he has redeemed his people. What is the right response to what God has done in love, without merit on the part of those chosen to be his people, whether it be the people of Israel or the New Testament Church?

Watch your sequence in reading the Old Testament — or the New!

God acts unilaterally in election or in redemption, as he does in the making of the covenant; but he has a purpose in mind always: he seeks a response from his people; they are expected to be *responsible,* and therefore to live as a people of God in fellowship and service, in faith and obedience; in short, to be worthy of the name *people of God.*

The Old Testament as well as the New is a story of God's grace, but it is *not cheap grace.* We saw it in the story of Abraham, who was called *to be a blessing*; and we remember how prominent the word *obedience* was in that story. Why should *we* be afraid of the word "obedience," or "response," or "responsible"? Watch your sequence in reading, we have said. God acts first, man is called to respond.

There are three striking statements of deep theological significance in the passage before us, all indicative of *responsibility* because of divine *redemption.*

"Now therefore, if you will obey my voice and keep my covenant:" that means if you are willing to obey the covenant requirements, and to be guided by the teaching of the Law and the Prophets into the knowledge of God's will and into submission thereto as a God-pleasing way of life. We speak in general terms right now; later on we shall spend a chapter on the Law and another on the Prophets. Right now the prayer in Psalm 143: 8, 10 may point up what we mean:

"Let me hear in the morning of thy steadfast love,
    for in thee I put my trust!
Teach me the way I should go,
    for to thee I lift up my soul.
Teach me to do thy will,
    for thou art my God!
Let thy good spirit lead me
    on a level path."

So do the prophet Samuel's words to his sinning people in I Samuel 12: 23, "Moreover as for me, far be it from me that I should sin against the LORD by ceasing to pray for you; and I will instruct you in the good and the right way." And so also does this prayer from our Sunday morning Service, "by thy Holy Spirit increase in us true knowledge of thee and of thy will, and true obedience to thy Word." Redemption, or salvation, is an act of grace; but no one can read the Scriptures honestly without being made aware that God is concerned with the response of obedience to his will and word and covenant.

A second statement is the promise, which is also a Commission, "and you shall be to me a kingdom of priests." The emphasis now is on *mission,* Israel's mission which relates so closely to Abraham's call to be a blessing. In terms of our theme we might call it Israel's mission to be a "Responsible People of God." It can be made more specific than that, however. Israel's function, as Franz Delitzsch, the great Old Testament commentator of the last century, once said was to be spiritual priests and kings in relation to all the peoples of the earth, which the LORD claims as his own. Priesthood suggests a spiritual act in behalf of someone. Kingship in this context denotes a spiritual rule over someone. The thing to be noted is that we again encounter the concept of servanthood, as in the call of Abraham to be a blessing of which this is a continuation. Israel's relation to the LORD as "his very own" was never a selfish one. To them was given the function of sharing by word and deed the knowledge of "the living God" and of his revealed "new way of life." In *God's Covenant of Blessing* the present author makes this assertion: "The election of Israel and its vocation to be in a special sense the people of God is incomprehensible and indefensible apart from the covenant mission." This is what Gerhard von Rad said in essence about the particularism of the election of Abraham. It is true also of the Christian Church. It is a vital part of our Hebrew-Christian heritage. We are redeemed for a purpose. We are redeemed to be a Responsible People of God; and this implies a willingness to do the will of God the Redeemer, to be obedient to his teaching as to the good and right way of life, to keep his covenant by listening to his guiding voice in the Law and the Prophets, for our good always. It includes also a readiness to serve the LORD their God by accepting the Mission of being a blessing, a royal spiritual priesthood to the nations, so that *particularism* might evolve under God into *universalism*. Don't overlook the significant words, "for all the earth is mine." Only so can we understand the New Testament application of these words from Exodus in I Peter 2: 9, "But you are a chosen race, a royal priesthood, a holy nation, God's own people, that you may declare the wonderful deeds of him who called you out of darkness into his marvelous light." Such was the redemptive purpose of God with Israel. Such is his redemptive purpose on a far greater scale with all humanity through Jesus Christ. Through the exodus-redemption experience of Israel as interpreted by Moses God began to teach us all the great spiritual truth that to whom much has been given, of him shall much be required.

There is a third facet of our theme which involves the element of response. To be a Responsible People of God means to be "a holy nation" (RSV), "a sacred nation" (Moffat), "a consecrated nation" (Ronald Knox) : in short, to have a holy character. In what sense?

This is not the time and place for a thorough study of the concept of holiness in the Old Testament; but a few things must be said in addition to what was said in chapter one in connection with the holiness of God. Here the adjective *holy* is applied to a nation, to a people chosen by God to be his very own. By what right is it so used? We remember how Jesus answered the ruler who addressed him as "Good Teacher:" "Why do you call me good? No one is good but God alone." Must we not with equal if not even greater reason say, "No one is holy but God alone?" Certainly according to our Hebrew-Christian heritage God is "the Holy One of Israel." The Hebrew word, as we pointed out in chapter one, seems to suggest being set apart in transcendant glory and in aweful purity (Faber, My God, how wonderful thou art). As such it would seem to pertain to God alone; and to be in the presence of the Holy God is an awesome experience. The prophet Isaiah discovered that one day in the temple where a routine worship was turned into a vision of the thrice-holy living God (Isaiah 6). May I quote again the remarkable passage in Isaiah 57: 15, which I for one have learned to love because it combines the holiness and the compassionate love of God:

> "For thus says the high and lofty One
>> who inhabits eternity, whose name is Holy:
> 'I dwell in the high and holy place,
>> and also with him who is of a contrite and humble spirit,
> to revive the spirit of the humble,
>> and to revive the heart of the contrite.' "

God is holy. Of that there can be no doubt. He is holy in all his attributes, in mercy as well as might. He is perfect. He is totally other than man. To say that God is holy is to ascribe to him "essential Deity," with all the deep moral implications therein involved.

But if we define holiness in this way, as fundamentally an attribute of God, how can there be such a thing as "a holy nation," "a holy people," "a holy place," "a holy way of life"? What sense does it make for God to say as he does to Moses in Leviticus 19: 2, "Say to all the congregation of the people of Israel, You shall be holy; for I the LORD your God am holy"? You may remember that the New Testament not only quotes this admonition but enlarges upon it, in I Peter 1: 14-16. "As obedient children, do not be conformed to the passions of your former ignorance, but as he who called you is holy, be holy yourselves in all your conduct; since it is written, 'You shall be holy, for I am holy.' "

It makes sense only if you look at it in the light of the biblical doctrine of sanctification, which has a twofold thrust. A holy nation or people is a consecrated nation, which through God's act of redemption has been set apart as the possession of the holy God. It involves a God-given status, which includes also my commitment to him as his very own. For a holy nation is also one that is being transformed or renewed day by day into the likeness of the holiness of God. It is a nation set apart by God, but it is also a self-dedicated nation. This is what Christians through the ages have called the daily renewal of that image of God in which we were once created. We can readily see how closely redemption is related to creation: how it is aimed at the restoration of the image of God which was lost in the fall. We can see the beginning of the outline of God's ultimate redemptive purpose in the Old Testament, in a passage like Exodus 19: 3-6; but it is in the New Testament that we see this outline filled out and defined as primarily an act of God through Jesus Christ in our behalf. The proper response to divine redemption is that attitude of submission and of earnest seeking to know and do the will of God which is the mark of a holy nation, and therefore also of a Responsible People of God. However difficult, we must try to keep in proper balance God's act of grace in redemption and man's response in the renewal of life. Such has been the combination in our Hebrew-Christian heritage from the beginning, and still is today. We are Redeemed to be a Responsible People of God.

> "O Israel, hope in the LORD!
>   for with the LORD there is steadfast love,
>   and with him is plenteous redemption.
> And he will redeem Israel from all his iniquities."
>
> (Psalm 130; 7-8)

A Postscript: An Exodus Theology

We said earlier in the chapter that we would review in a concluding postscript Gustaf Wingren's book, *An Exodus Theology*. The book is well worth reading in connection with our theme of Redemption. We shall attempt only a brief resumé.

Wingren's aim is to acquaint English readers with the theology of a relatively unknown but nevertheless highly influential Swedish theologian by the name of Einar Billing, who lived in the years 1871-1939.

Billing's theology was essentially a theology of the Old Testament; that is, the Old Testament was the starting point for his biblical theology, which of course included the New Testament as well.

Billing's emphasis, as with G. Ernest Wright, Eric Wahlstrom, Robert Marshall, myself, and others, was on "the God who acts:" in events, but also in the spoken word.

The pattern for his Old Testament theology as "An Exodus Theology" was the Exodus-liberation from Egypt.

His New Testament interpretation followed a similar pattern: an exodus in a new and completely personal form through the work of Jesus Christ.

This biblical pattern of exodus merges into the history of the Christian Church, whose task is to open the way to an "exodus" for all humanity through the proclamation of the forgiveness of sins.

In other words, for Einar Billing the key to the interpretation of the Scriptures and of our Hebrew-Christian heritage was the concept of "exodus," beginning with the exodus-redemption of Israel from Egypt in which Billing sees not only historical but theological significance.

We may disagree with him in details; but nevertheless *there is an Exodus Theology*, just as there is a Covenant Theology (which I personally prefer as the key-concept in biblical interpretation): two fundamental theological viewpoints never to be separated one from the other, no matter with which we choose to begin our study of the bible, two theo-

71

logical viewpoints not only inseparable from each other but serving to bind the Old Testament and the New Testament together in one unified whole. For the God who acts in redemption does so with a view to achieving an eternal relationship of Covenant. The words of Exodus 19: 3-6 come to mind again: "You have seen — how I brought you to myself — to be my very own." This is the purpose of the exodus. This is the purpose of redemption. This is the purpose finally of Covenant.

Chapter 6

THE CONCEPT OF TORAH AND COVENANT

Once more we shall overlap considerably what we have already said, especially in chapter 5 concerning a Responsible People of God. In fact, insofar as we link the concepts of Torah and Covenant we also overlap what we have said about the Covenant of Blessing with Abraham and the discussion of the Covenant in Exodus 19: 3-6. Our primary concern, however, is with the Torah or the Law, within the framework of the Covenant with Israel.

The concept of the Torah is, if I may say so, both a very concrete and a highly complex concept. It has been the subject of much misunderstanding and misinterpretation; or perhaps we should say, the subject of varying interpretation and of provocative questions.

I.

There are, for example, especially these three significant questions. (There are more, but we shall limit ourselves to these three.)

1. In the New Testament we read this statement in John 1: 17, "For the law was given through Moses; grace and truth came through Jesus Christ." The words of the statement seem simple enough; but what do they really mean? We are not yet discussing the true meaning of the Hebrew word Torah, but take it in its usually accepted sense of Law. Does the statement in John 1: 17 imply that Moses, and indeed the whole Old Testament, was concerned only with the Law and not at all with the Gospel? Does it imply that Jesus Christ, and indeed the whole New Testament, is concerned only with the Gospel, with grace and truth, and not at all with the Law and the Commandments? Does the Old Testament teach salvation by works of the Law, and the New Testament salvation by grace through faith? If we interpret the statement in strictly literal terms it might seem so. There are some theologians who speak just that way. But already in our study of our Hebrew-Christian heritage we have seen that there is no such sharp cleavage between the Old Testament and

the New. The contrast in John 1: 17 is *relative,* not absolute. There is Law and Gospel throughout the Bible. Moses spoke the beautiful words in Exodus 34: 6-7a, "The LORD passed before him, and proclaimed, 'The LORD, the LORD, a God merciful and gracious, slow to anger, and abounding in steadfast love and faithfulness, keeping steadfast love for thousands, forgiving iniquity and transgression and sin — :" It is in the Old Testament that we find the familiar words:

> "If thou, O LORD, shouldst mark iniquities,
>   Lord, who could stand?
> But there is forgiveness with thee,
>   that thou mayest be feared." (Psalm 130: 3-4)

And it was Jesus who preached the Sermon on the Mount, with its heart-searching application of the demands of the Law. The Augustana Catechism of 1939 correctly says that "The Bible is divided as to its contents into the law and the gospel;" but this division does not coincide with the division into the Old and the New Testaments. There is rather a sense in which every word of God contains an element of Law as well as of Gospel.

2. A second New Testament statement that has often been misinterpreted is found in Romans 3: 20, "For no human being will be justified in his sight by works of the law since through the law comes knowledge of sin." It is certainly true that no one will be justified in God's sight by obedience to the Law. If this were not so, why spend all the time that we did in chapter 5 on the concept of Redemption *as an act of God* which precedes any human response in the form of either faith or obedience? It is certainly true that "through the law comes the knowledge of sin." Luther's familiar illustration of the Law as a mirror in which we see ourselves as we are and as we ought to be comes to mind. But is that its only, or even its primary, purpose? How then explain the psalmist's words, "Oh, how I love thy law! It is my meditation all the day."? How explain the words of the Deuteronomist, "And now, Israel, what does the LORD your God require of you but to fear the LORD your God, to walk in all his ways, to love him, to serve the LORD your God with all your heart and with all your soul, and to keep the commandments and statutes of the LORD, *which I command you this day for your good?"* There is, as we shall see, another significant function of the Law besides the conviction of sin. And it is not only the Law that leads to the conviction of sin. See, for example, Romans 2: 4b, "Do you not know that God's kindness is meant to lead you to repentance?" Consider also the second stanza of the hymn "Beneath the Cross of Jesus":

"Upon the cross of Jesus,
    Mine eye at times can see
The very dying form of One
    Who suffered there for me.
And from my smitten heart with tears,
    These wonders I confess, —
The wonder of His glorious love,
    And my own worthlessness."

Surely there is no better way to know the depth of our sinfulness than when confronted by the greatness of his redeeming love on the Cross! And God's requirements, if taken seriously, may hit us hard, but they also guide us in a good way. Of that we shall say more later.

3. A third question which has been much discussed, though not based on any specific bible passage, is whether the Law relates to Creation or to Redemption. There is a sense in which God gave his Law when he made man obedient to his will at creation. This is the law written in the heart and conscience of man, of which Paul speaks in Romans 2: 14-16. Among others Gustaf Wingren stresses this aspect in *Creation and the Law*. But the Old Testament concept of Torah (the Hebrew word usually translated "law") is more directly related to the theme of the saving acts of God as seen in Election, Redemption, Covenant, the People of God relationship: with a Mission as well as a Blessing, because called not only to fellowship but to servanthood; or as we saw in chapter 5, called to be a Responsible People of God. In terms of the history of Israel it belongs under the Covenant, and a good biblical base for discussion is Exodus 19-24.

II.

Seen in this setting of the history of Israel, what do we mean by the Law or the Torah (the Hebrew word)? Something must be said by way of definition and description before we speak of its specific place in the scheme of biblical theology and of our Hebrew-Christian heritage.

1. What is the Law? The *Augustana Catechism of 1939* says this, "The law is God's command that we be holy in heart and life." That may be too simplistic a definition, but it is at least partly true. The Law is a command, or a series of commandments, not a promise, or a series of promises. It is a requirement in which God sets forth what man should do, not a declaration of what God has done or will do. It calls for conformity to God's will in heart and life. We remember the penitential prayer in our Sunday morning Service, wherein we pray not only for the forgiveness of

sins but also for increase in the true knowledge of God and of his will, and for true obedience to his word.

2. In the *Westminster Dictionary of the Bible* we find another answer to the question, What is the law? We are told that it is "an authoritative rule of conduct" (art, Law), which "presents the commandments and claims of Yahweh to man" (art. Wisdom). Again the definition may seem too simplistic, but it is helpful to an understanding of the Torah. It is a rule of conduct which presents the claims of God upon us: the God who has redeemed us to be his people. That was true in the case of Israel. It is also true of us. Any discussion of the Law apart from the preceding act of God in redemption is nonsensical. It is the act of God in redemption which gives authority to the Torah. Does he not have the right to tell "his very own" what to do: and cannot the Redeemer be trusted to require only that which is good for his redeemed?

3. But let us try a third approach to the question, What is the Law? Let us consider the Hebrew word *Torah* which is generally translated *law.* At least that is true up to and including the Revised Standard Version of the Old Testament. It is so translated throughout the American Standard Version.

The actual meaning of *Torah,* however, is divine *Teaching.* It is so translated, and correctly so, by RSV in Isaiah 8: 16, 20, "Bind up the testimony, seal the teaching among my disciples. — To the teaching and to the testimony!" It is true that the reference here is to prophetic teaching, but the word is Torah; and ASV translates it as *law.*

W. A. Whitehouse has a very good discussion of the word in Richardson's *A Theoretical Word Book of the Bible*: "*Torah* denotes the guidance or instruction which comes from God through the oracular utterances of the priests or through the prophets; it is the whole content of God's revelation of his nature and purpose, which incidentally makes clear man's responsibility before God. In so far as this responsibility is clarified by a collection of maxims into a legislative code, the term may be applied to such a code —. The LXX translators understood most of the Old Testament references to *torah* in this sense, and supplies the translation *nomos*, which passed into New Testament thought and into our English Bibles as 'law,' creating thereby a misleading impression of the way God had dealt with Israel to make them his people. It obscures the wider and more personal communication which is partly suggested by 'teaching,' and implies that Israel is bound to God in a relation which is adequately expressed by strict obedience to a code of law." According to this article the primary emphasis in *Torah* is on guidance or teaching rather than on a written code of law.

This is also the viewpoint of A. B. Davidson in *The Theology of the Old Testament*: "The law was given to the people in covenant. It was a rule of life, not of justification; it was a guide to the man who was already right in God's esteem in virtue of his general attitude towards the covenant. The law is not to Israel a law of morals on the bare ground of human duty, apart from God's exhibition of his grace. It is a line marked out along which the life of the people or the person in covenant with God, and already right with God on that ground, is to unfold itself."

A good example of the use of *Torah* in the sense of *Teaching* is found in the latest Jewish version of The Torah (the first five books of the Bible), 1962. See, for example, Deuteronomy 1: 5, "On the other side of the Jordan, in the land of Moab, Moses undertook to expound this Teaching." Anyone who is at all acquainted with the book of Deuteronomy will recall that the word *Torah* is one of the key-words to the book.

Perhaps you begin to see the pattern in my own interpretation in the preceding chapters, which I have equated with our Hebrew-Christian heritage. The starting point for the first three chapters was *the creative act of God*, which placed man in a unique relationship with his Maker. On the basis of that unique relationship he was called to obedience to the will of God. But man sinned by disobedience, and the unique relationship with God was broken. Then as a new starting point we noted *the saving acts of God*, which were expressed in terms of election, redemption, covenant, a Responsible People of God, with a mission to be a blessing to all the families of the earth. The significant thing is that God always acts first. What we have said about *Torah* or Teaching or Law in this chapter is always by way of response to the redemptive act of God. The Torah belongs under the Covenant, or of the relationship of the People of God to their Redeemer. It expresses God's guidance, and man's response to that guidance. It is indicative of the good and gracious as well as the righteous will of God. It is motivated by divine grace, not by "a written code" (II Corinthians 3: 6 and context). This is not to deny its function as convicting of sin; but it combines with it the picture of a heavenly father whose Teaching is meant to lead his very own in a good and a right way. Not until we see these two functions of the Torah will we understand what is meant by the Law in our Hebrew-Christian heritage. And of these two, the primary functon is Teaching the will of God as to the rght way in

77

which his people should walk, or what the prophet Samuel calls "the good and the right way" (I Samuel 12: 23) and what the prophet Jeremiah calls simply "the good way" (Jeremiah 6: 16): the way of life for a redeemed people of God. The prophet Isaiah puts it succinctly: "This is the way, walk in it" (Isaiah 30: 21). The psalmist prayed: "Teach me the way I should go, for to thee I lift up my soul" (Psalm 143: 8b). In the New Testament Christianity was at first called the Way (Acts 24: 14, 22). This does not deny the secondary function of the Torah or the Law: to convict of sin whenever we stray from the way. The Hebrew Torah always functions in these two ways for God's people. Why should it not? They need both!

III.

But what is then the content of the Law in its totality: "the law of Moses," the Torah, the Law in the Pentateuch?

The real Bible student quickly discovers the complexity or diversity in unity at this point. Let us note the contents briefly, though we cannot spend too much time here.

For example:

1. There are three Codes of law in the Pentateuch; though the Teaching element is not altogether excluded even here, and the connection with the saving acts of God in history is evident.

The first Code is the Book of the Covenant; see Exodus 24:7. This Code includes Exodus 21-23, or perhaps Exodus 20-24. It is the oldest Code in the Old Testament, and we shall outline it before concluding this chapter.

The second Code is the Law of Holiness. It includes Leviticus 17-26. It is ritual or cultic in character. If we speak of Mosaic authorship it would have to be in terms of "essential Mosaicity"; it was a growing, living law, which allows for a history of development.

The third Code is the Deuteronomic Code. It includes Deuteronomy 12-26. It is commonly assumed that it was inspired by the spirit of the first of the great prophets. It gives the impression of being an attempt to apply the spirit of the older law to a new situation. The Teaching element is to the fore in many parts of this Code.

2. In terms of our Hebrew-Christian heritage we are more concerned about *three facets* of the Old Testament Law than we are about the three Codes. We enumerate them first, then we shall analyze them carefully on the basis of Exodus 20-23.

The first is what may be called *moral* law. A good illustration is the Ten Commandments. They are *apodictic* in character: the language is that of a direct command or prohibition, "thou shalt" or "thou shalt not." There is no "if" or "when" attached, to give the commandment or the prohibition anything resembling a *conditional* character. They express God's unconditional will as to what ought or ought not to be done.

The second is what may be called *ritual* or *ceremonial* law. It is cultic in character, having to do with forms of worship. The best example is the Law of Holiness in the book of Leviticus; but there is one significant illustration in the Book of the Covenant, which we shall examine later.

The third is what may be called *civil* law. This is where the principles of the moral law are applied to actual life situations, sometimes with penalties attached where the law is violated. It is primarily under the civil law that we find the conditional "if" or "when," implying that violations did actually occur and legislating what should then be done. The best example is in Exodus 21-23, and in some portions of Deuteronomy.

IV.

Let us now examine the three facets of the Law on the basis of the significant passage in Exodus 19-24. Our chief concern is with the *moral* content of the Torah, because this is most relevant to our Hebrew-Christian heritage; the *ritual* and the *civil* possess what we may call a local "times-coloring," being directed primarily to the people of Israel, and having for us primarily a symbolic significance. The principle, but not necessarily the letter, applies today. In this sense the *ritual* and the *civil* law can be seen to have sometimes a basically timeless relevance; but the *moral* law is in its very nature an expression of the timeless will of God for his people.

The introduction to the Book of the Covenant we have already studied in part in Exodus 19. We recall the saving acts of God, especially the reference in verse 4 to the exodus-redemption. We recall also the basic principles of the covenant, both as looking backward to the covenant with Abraham and forward to the ratification of this covenant with Israel. We recall the theophany: the meeting with the living God who is holy, and who not only acts redemptively in behalf of his people but also speaks to this redeemed people his will for them as a Responsible People of God. Everything that follows from Exodus 19 on must be seen within this framework of redemption, and in relation to the concept of the living God who both acts and speaks: by whose act we are made his people and by whose speech we are guided to live as his people ought to live.

The supreme illustration of the moral law in the Old Testament is the Decalogue or the Ten Commandments. They are recorded almost verbatim twice, in Exodus 20: 1-17 and in Deuteronomy 5: 1-21. Actually they are not called "ten commandments" but "ten words" (see Exodus 34: 28, RSV footnote). There are various ways of numbering them, but this does not concern our present purpose. We do note, however, that one of the most significant "words" is the preamble in Exodus 20: 2, "I am the LORD your God, who brought you out of the land of Egypt, out of the house of bondage." This wonderful declarative statement of God's redeeming grace helps us to get the proper perspective for the Ten Commandments. They were spoken to a people who were already God's "very own," made so by God's redeeming grace. There is no thought here of *earning status* with God by keeping the commandments. The Redeemer simply points out that a relationship such as he had created between himself and Israel gave him the right to direct his people *in the right way*. Do you remember how Paul moves from his wonderful proclamation of the mercies of God in Romans 1-8 to the admonitions as to Christian conduct or behavior in Romans 12ff? The key-word is the adverb "therefore" in Romans 12: 1. You can just as legitimately insert this adverb between verses 2 and 3 in Exodus 20. That is, all the commandments issue as a *Teaching guide* from the exodus-redemption experience. If we apply them to ourselves as Christians they issue from "the mercies of God" as experienced in Jesus Christ. They are *good* commandments. They were given, says the author of Deuteronomy, "for your good" (Deuteronomy 12: 13). They are a guide, says the prophet Samuel, "in the good and the right way" (I Samuel 12: 23). Luther in his Small Catechism links all the commandments with a right fear and love of God: that is, if we rightly fear and love God there are certain things that we will do and certain things that we will not do in every area covered by one of the commandments. There is nothing legalistic about the Decalog *if* we see it in its proper redemptive perspective and *if* we have a proper understanding of *Torah* as divine *Teaching*.

Of course, the commandments had a peculiar significance for Israel as the Old Testament people of God. They were, says the *Westminster Dictionary of the Bible,* "the fundamental laws of the Hebrew state," comparable to the English Magna Carta or to our American Constitution. They were conceived of as expressing "a covenant between God and the nation." They are also, according to the same Bible Dictionary, "a summary of the whole moral code — founded in the immutable nature of God and in the permanent relations of men on earth." There is nothing "iffy" about the Ten Commandments according to our Hebrew-Christian heritage. They are an enduring expression of God's will for the life of his people. They can of course be simplified and summarized, as Jesus did in answer to the lawyer's question, "Teacher, which is the great commandment in the law?" Jesus refused to choose between them. Instead he summed up the teaching of the entire Decalog in two commandments which covered a right relationship with God and with our neighbor: "You shall love the Lord your God with all your heart, and with all your soul, and with all your mind. This is the great and first commandment. And a second is like it, You shall love your neighbor as yourself. On these two commandments depend all the law and the prophets." (Matthew 22: 37-40). There was nothing original about Jesus' summation in this fashion. The two commandments to which he refers are found in the Old Testament, in Deuteronomy 6: 4-5 and Leviticus 19: 18; but even without them, a careful study of the Ten Commandments will reveal exactly this same twofold emphasis on love for God and for our neighbor. They are more than a legal code. They represent the intensely personal teaching of a loving God aimed at the welfare of his people; for no one can ignore the responsibility of love for God or neighbor without suffering the loss of a right relationship to both God and men. At the heart of the Torah or the Law is God's will that we love one another, even as God has loved us. In Romans 13: 10 Paul summarizes the law in a single word: love. There are other words, not unrelated to love, which are equally good as a summary of the law or of the requirements of God. See, for example, the parable of the vineyard in Isaiah 5: 1-7, especially verse 7:

> "For the vineyard of the LORD of hosts
>   is the house of Israel,
> and the men of Judah
>   are his pleasant planting;
> and he looked for justice,
>   but behold, bloodshed;
> for righteousness,
>   but behold, a cry!"

The Old Testament, and our Hebrew-Christian heritage, has much to say about justice, as it does also about mercy. Who shall say that either is irrelevant in today's world or to Christianity as we know it? The fact that God's people, both Israel and the Christian Church, have all too often failed to manifest justice or mercy does not alter the fact that each has a vital place in our Hebrew-Christian heritage. So does the Golden Rule as Jesus taught it in the Sermon on the Mount: "So whatever you wish that men would do to you, do so to them; for this is the law and the prophets." (Matthew 7: 12). So does the fruit of the Spirit so beautifully expressed in Galatians 5: 22-23, in contrast to the preceding works of the flesh: "But the fruit of the Spirit is love, joy, peace, patience, kindness, goodness, faithfulness, gentleness, self-control; against such there is no law." There is more than a superficial connection between the next verse and the purpose of the Torah seen as divine Teaching for "God's very own": "And those who belong to Christ Jesus have crucified the flesh with its passions and desires." What we are concerned about is the will of God for his chosen people. Paul puts it well when he says in Romans 12: 2, "Do not be conformed to this world but be transformed by the renewal of your mind, that you may prove what is the will of God, what is good and acceptable and perfect." The moral law has to do with the will of God for his people. As such Martin Luther interprets the Ten Commandments in his Small Catechism. As such we accept it as a fundamental part of our Hebrew-Christian heritage.

The Ritual Law

The moral law is immutable as the expression of God's will for men whom he created and redeemed to be his very own. It is an unchangeable part of our Hebrew-Christian heritage. Can the same be said for the Old Testament ritual law?

The answer is an emphatic No, both from the Jewish and from the Christian point of view. For the modern Jew the destruction of the temple made it impossible to practice the Old Testament cultic worship. A new form of worship took its place, centered in the synagogue, with Scripture reading and prayer as its chief component parts. For today's Christian the Old Testament worship has been abrogated or set aside. One of the clearest testimonies to this effect is found in Hebrews 7: 18, 19, "On the one hand, a former commandment is set aside because of its weakness and uselessness (for the law made nothing perfect): on the other hand, a better hope is introduced, through which we draw near to God." That the reference is to the law of worship, or to the cultic law, is confirmed by Hebrews 10: 1, "For since the law has but a shadow of the good things to come instead of the true form of these realities, it can never, by the same sacrifices which are continually offered year after year, make perfect those who draw near." If it were necessary we could quote from the Pauline letters to the same effect. Our concern, however, is with another question: Did the Old Testament law of worship, the ritual law, have any significance for our Hebrew-Christian heritage; and if so, what was it?

The answer can be found in Exodus 20: 21-26, where we have the basic principles of worship which are found in expanded form in the latter part of Exodus and in Leviticus. We are not concerned with the letter of the ritual law, but only with its basic principles; for it is these which have a symbolic and a theological value for our Hebrew-Christian heritage. We recall the fear created by the theophany and the people's request for some one to serve as a mediator. In response the LORD provided what we may call *a way of access* for his people in worship. There is a theological basis consisting first in God's initiative in coming to his people and speaking to them (verse 22); and then in a backward reference to the moral law in the Ten Commandments (verse 23). You have here the same double affirmation with which the Decalogue begins: that God is One, and that God is Spirit, and therefore he cannot be represented by any idol made of silver or gold. Without this confession there can be no true worship in the sense in which it has been understood for thousands of years in our Hebrew-Christian heritage. True worship is based on true theology. As Jesus said to the Samaritan woman, "God is spirit, and those who worship him must worship in spirit and truth" (John 4: 24).

Another principle of worship in the Old Testament is its sacrificial character. We have a brief allusion to this in Exodus 20: 24, with a detailed development in Leviticus. This sacrificial aspect of worship was as definitely a part of the Old Testament Torah as was the moral law. It was a God-appointed way of access through which they were taught the need of atonement for sin if they were to come into God's presence. Even in the Old Testament its primary significance was symbolic. According to the New Testament, as we have seen, it has been disannulled or set aside. Or perhaps it would be more accurate to say that it has been fulfilled in the perfect sacrifice of Jesus Christ for the sins of the world. As *ritual* it has no further significance; yet, as a part of our Hebrew-Christian heritage it was instrumental in teaching the truth so clearly stated in Hebrews 9: 22, "without the shedding of blood there is no forgiveness of sins." In itself it was only a shadow of the good things to come, but even now the symbolic significance of this shadow helps us to appreciate the reality of the substance that has come *through the offering of the body of Jesus Christ once for all* (Hebrews 10: 10). In spite of "its weakness and uselessness" (for the law made nothing perfect), it *was* a shadow of the good things to come; and we thank God for this preparatory lesson given unto Israel to guide them in the essential principles of worship.

Another such principle is found in the latter part of Exodus 20: 24, "in every place where I cause my name to be remembered I will come to you and bless you." Worship is a meeting between man and God, but in that meeting God takes the initiative. Worship is a response to an act or to a word of God. It was so when God met Moses in the awesome theophany of the burning bush. It was so in every moment of God's intervention in history which we have called election. It was so when he appointed "the mercy seat" for his people Israel and said to Moses, "There I will meet you, and from above the mercy seat, from between the two cherubim that are upon the ark of the testimony, I will speak with you of all that I will give you in commandment for the people of Israel" (Exodus 25: 22). The New Testament counterpart for "the mercy seat" is "the throne of grace" to which we may draw near with confidence in our worship of prayer and praise because God has willed it so (Hebrews 4: 16). In a deeper sense God initiates this meeting with man in worship when ever he draws near to his people *in the proclamation of his word.* There can be no true worship unless we permit God to speak to us before we exercise our God-given privilege of drawing near to speak to him.

There is one additional principle of worship in the Old Testament, not mentioned in Exodus 20: 21-26, which is an essential part of our Hebrew-Christian heritage. We refer to the great religious festivals which celebrated significant faith-events in Israel's history. Among them are the feast of passover and of unleavened bread, the feast of tabernacles or booths, the feast of weeks, and the annual day of atonement. A similar list in the New Testament and in the history of the Christian Church would be Christmas, the feast of Epiphany, Lent, Good Friday, Easter, and Pentecost. We shall not go into details but rather confine ourselves to the principle of the thing; letting this statement from Deuteronomy 16: 16 interpret the basic signfiicance of such events in relation to worship, and indirectly to our Hebrew-Christian heritage: "Three times a year all your males shall appear before the LORD your God at the place which he will choose: at the feast of unleavened bread, at the feast of weeks, and at the feast of booths. They shall not appear before the LORD empty-handed; every man shall give as he is able, according to the blessing of the LORD your God which he has given you." The emphasis, you will note, is three-fold: 1) a coming into the presence of the Lord 2) at the place of his choice, and implied at least 3) in thankful response for his blessings or to his saving act of grace. Beyond this we need not go.

The Civil Law

By civil law we mean the ordinances or judgments (Hebrew *mishpatim*) which represent the application of the principles of the Torah in the sense of moral law to a given historical situation or set of circumstances. In the Book of the Covenant chapters 21-23 are essentially civil law. You will note their essentially hypothetical character: that is, they are usually introduced by the conjunctions "when" or "if," or perhaps by the pronoun "whoever." Visualize the situation. If it should happen, contrary to the Torah in its absolute moral sense, and contrary to the character of Israel as God's own people and a holy nation, that certain offenses occurred the civil law laid down certain concrete rules for handling the situation. The civil law did not necessarily move on the same high level as the moral law, though both belonged to the Torah as given to Israel. Shall we say that the civil law recognized the fact of human imperfection, and dealt with the human situation accordingly. We might even go further and admit that the civil law was in itself imperfect. It often sought to regulate the existing situation rather than to insist on the ideal principle. That is why certain practices such as polygamy and slavery were not immediately uprooted. The civil laws of Israel were geared to the historical and social milieu of that day and place. They were largely pastoral or agricultural in character, since that was the character of society in ancient Israel. No literal application to our industrialized society would be possible, even if the laws themselves were perfect, which some of them are not. But some principles shine through that are relevant even today. For example, the law in Exodus 21: 33-34, which forbade leaving an open pit lest someone's animal fall into it and be hurt, and which provided for compensation when the law was violated, is in harmony with today's accident or negligence compensation laws. So also the law of restitution in Exodus 22: 5-6 for loss inflicted on another's property is certainly ethically justifiable. It is also easy to see why our Hebrew-Christian heritage should stress the law against false witness recorded in Exodus 23: 1-3. The law in Exodus 23: 4-5 that we should help to rescue the ox or ass even of an enemy is simply a concrete illustration of Jesus' teaching that we should love even our enemies; see Matthew 5: 43ff. Though we may question whether Exodus 22: 16 is always the best answer where a woman has been seduced, and though we may think that capital punishment is unduly severe for such crimes as sorcery (Exodus 22: 18), or unnatural sex acts (Exodus 22: 19), or worship of other gods (Exodus 22: 20), it is nevertheless true that through the civil law of the Old Testament as a whole there runs a concern for justice and mercy, and an emphasis on our duty to God and man, which is not commonly found in the laws of antiquity. But over and above all we have the moral law which perfectly expresses God's will for man whom he has created and redeemed; and it is this moral law which constitutes the heart of the Torah as well as of our Hebrew-Christian heritage.

The LORD's Covenant with Israel

Exodus 1-18 is primarily a redemption experience and an exodus theology. Exodus 19-24 is primarily concerned with the making of the covenant with Israel and with a covenant theology. The two belong together, though we have chosen to study them separately. Since the Torah is a fundamental part of the covenant we end this chapter in our Hebrew-Christian heritage by noting the formal establishment of the Lord's Covenant with Israel in Exodus 24.

In relation to the promise and commission given to Abraham, which is also called a covenant, what we have here might be called *a covenant renewal*. The covenant with Abraham from the very beginning included also his descendants. In that sense the word covenant is used in Exodus 19: 4-6; but at this stage in the history of Israel, after their redemption from slavery in Egypt, the covenant is formally ratified with them as a people at Sinai. The ratification ceremony has considerable significance for us, who think of God's dealings with Israel as a type of things to come in the New Testament Church.

Two things in particular were significant in this ratification ceremony. The one was an act of sacrifice, made by young men chosen by Moses to represent the people of Israel in offering burnt offerings and peace offerings to the LORD. This "blood of the covenant" was then sprinkled in two directions: half of it against the altar, and half of it upon the people. The sprinkling was accompanied by this word from Moses, "Behold the blood of the covenant which the LORD has made with you in accordance with all these words" (Exodus 24: 8). The "words" to which he refers are those written in "the book of the covenant" which Moses read in the hearing of the people as "the words of the LORD." To these words the people gave assent, saying, "All the words which the LORD has spoken we will do." Of course the promise was too glibly given,

86

and of course they failed often in the promised performance; but this does not alter the fact that what was spoken to them was the good and gracious and righteous will of God for them as his people. It is from this perspective that we must regard the Torah and the covenant based on it, both for the Jew and later for the Christian. It is obvious that both "the blood of the covenant" and "the book of the covenant" move in two directions: first, there is the act of God in commanding and receiving the sacrifice and in speaking the words of the covenant, then there is the human response to this act of God. Any attempt to reverse the order is fatal to our understanding of our Hebrew-Christian heritage. It is the LORD who makes the covenant. It is the LORD who speaks the words that are meant to guide his people in the good and the right way. It is the LORD who ordains the sacrifice on which all future access to the mercy seat was based. As a Jewish scholar once said about Exodus 24, "This transaction was the most important in the whole history of Israel. By this one sacrifice, never renewed, Israel was formally set apart as the people of God, and it lay at the foundation of all the sacrificial worship which followed. — Thus this one sacrifice prefigured the one sacrifice of our Lord Jesus Christ for his Church, which is the ground of our access to God and the foundation of all our worship and service." This is perfectly right as far as "the blood of the covenant" is concerned; but don't overlook "the book of the covenant" or the fact that God made the covenant "in accordance with all these words." This has been the theme of this chapter; and if we have grasped it clearly perhaps we can begin to understand the psalmist's exclamation, and to say with him, "Oh, how I love thy law (thy teaching, thy will)! It is my meditation all the day." Psalm 119: 97.

Chapter 7

THE CONCEPT OF PROPHECY

There is a close connection between the concept of prophecy and that of Torah or the Law in our Hebrew-Christian heritage. We shall try to clarify the connection as well as the distinction as we study the concept of prophecy. Both proclaim the will of God for his people; sometimes in the form of commandments and prohibitions, sometimes in the form of promises. For the Torah in the sense of the first five books of the Old Testament includes the promise to Abraham as well as the book of the covenant with Israel. That is to say, it includes both law and promise; and in the promise is contained a prophecy which found its ultimate fulfillment in Christ and in the New Testament people of God. We do not suggest that the distinction between law and gospel, or between commandment and promise, is not a valid one; but we do suggest that the distinction is not nearly as sharp as we sometimes make it out to be: that both law and gospel are parts of the one word of God which proclaims his total will for our salvation and also for our manner of life.

Right now, however, we are thinking especially of prophecy as a part of that one word of God. The New Testament quite frequently refers to "the law and the prophets" as if they together represented the sum total of the teaching of the Old Testament. Jesus says in Matthew 5: 17, "Think not that I have come to abolish the law and the prophets; I have come not to abolish them but to fulfill them." He uses the same terminology in the Golden Rule in Matthew 7: 12; and in speaking about the two great commandments of love for God and for our neighbor he says in Matthew 22: 40, "On these two commandments depend all the law and the prophets." Paul uses similar language in Romans 3: 21. In Acts 13: 15 "the reading of the law and the prophets" is seen to have been a fundamental part of worship in the Jewish synagogue.

Let me at this point make the comment that the concept of prophecy is fully as complex as that of the Torah or the Law. It may even seem slightly ridiculous to try to treat it in a study limited to a single chapter;

and of course, what we shall say will have value only as it may stimulate us to further study. We shall try to keep the presentation here as simple as possible, with fewer introductory questions and briefer answers, in order that we may have room for considerable illustration of the content of prophecy as a part of our Hebrew-Christian heritage. And as a keynote to the discussion may I ask you to read thoughtfully this New Testament quotation from II Peter 1: 19-21: "And we have the prophetic word made more sure. You will do well to pay attention to this as to a lamp shining in a dark place, until the day dawns and the morning star rises in your hearts. First of all you must understand this, that no prophecy of scripture is a matter of one's own interpretation, because no prophecy ever came by the impulse of man, but men moved by the Holy Spirit spoke from God."

Who Is a True Prophet?

Pay attention to the prophetic word (RSV), the word of prophecy (ASV). Why so? Or perhaps even more important as a first question, *who is* a true prophet in the Hebrew-Christian sense of the term that we should pay attention to him?

For in speaking of prophets and prophecy we need to watch our language carefully. "Prophets there have been in other religions and in other times," says John Paterson in *The Goodly Fellowship of the Prophets*. Even the Old Testament speaks of false prophets as well as true; of prophets of Baal as well as of Yahweh; of self-seeking prophets as well as dedicated spokesmen for the LORD God of Israel. How could their contemporaries tell the difference? For that matter, *how can we* tell the difference? Of that we shall say more after a while. Right now we face the question of definition: how do we define a true prophet, and how do we explain the function of prophecy, as these terms came to be used in our Hebrew-Christian heritage?

Let me submit a number of definitions, each supplementary to the other.

One of the simplest, and therefore one of the best, definitions of a true prophet is found in *The Westminster Dictionary of the Bible*: a prophet is "an authoritative and infallible teacher of God's will." Certainly such was the conviction of the biblical prophets themselves. We see it in their repeated use of the statement, "Thus says the LORD." We see it in what is sometimes called "the prophetic formula": "the word of the LORD came." They claimed to know the mind of the LORD. Therefore they claimed authority for their word over the conscience of Israel as the people of the LORD.

Quite similar is the definition of John Paterson in the book previously mentioned, *The Goodly Fellowship of the Prophets*: "To the Hebrew the prophet was one who spoke on behalf of God and interpreted the divine will. His word was not his own; it was the word of Jehovah who called him and gave him the word to speak."

In his Study Guide, *The Mighty Acts of God,* Robert Marshall defines "special revelation" in a way that relates it both to history and to prophecy, though he does not use these words: "Such revelation always included two elements, (1) a special event and (2) a special person or persons to interpret the event. Thus in the Bible God is revealed in the events of history interpreted by those gifted with special insight." In other words, the prophets were God's interpreters of the history of his people; or, if you will, interpreters of the acts of God.

Claude Tresmontant, in *A Study of Hebrew Thought,* also relates history and prophecy: "It is a characteristic of biblical history that those who carry it forward are made aware of its direction through the teachings of the prophets." Of this close connection between prophecy and history we shall say more in chapter 8, when we discuss the concept of history in our Hebrew-Christian heritage.

Another definition of prophecy is given by O. S. Rankin in *A Theological Word Book of the Bible,* edited by Alan Richardson: "The prophecy of the writing prophets, as this appears to us from the time of Amos onwards, takes the form of a declaration of the will or thought of Yahwah." We might add that the same is true of the non-writing prophets before the time of Amos, men such as Samuel, Elijah, and Elisha.

We might add one more quotation, which at the same time *concludes* this section on definition and *introduces* the next section on the primary function of the true prophet. The article on "Wisdom" in *The Westminster Dictionary of the Bible* discusses three departments of knowledge among the Hebrews. It makes this distinction between the law and prophecy: "The law presents the commandments and claims of Jehovah to man; prophecy passes judgment on conduct in the light of God's revealed will and explains the object of God's dealings with men." We might put it this way: prophecy applies the basic principles of the law to new circumstances and continues to reveal the will of God in its dynamic significant for the present situation.

Prophecy: Preaching or Prediction?

Our next question concerns the primary function of the true prophet: was it preaching or prediction?

Personally I would have to say that it was both. It is true that the preaching element of prophecy has often been overlooked. It is also true that the element of prediction has often been overemphasized. Yet both are an essential part of our Hebrew-Christian heritage. John Paterson in *The Goodly Fellowship of the Prophets* has put it well when he says: "The prophet was one who spoke for God and declared the intention of the divine heart; he made plain the purpose of God. That purpose concerned both the present and the future, and in that sense the prophet was both a forth-teller and a fore-teller. — Insight here implies foresight, for insight into the purposes and plan of God gives men knowledge of what God will do." Claude Tresmontant in *A Study of Hebrew Thought* has a similar and yet slightly different interpretation: "But the prophet does not see history, stretched out before him like a map, from which he need only pick out individual future events. Such foresight is not the prophet's gift. Rather he sees in which direction events are flowing. This is the scope of prophecy. The Hebrew conception of time excludes any other explanation of it." In the same manner O. S. Rankin says that "no hard and fast distinction can be drawn between prophecy as forthtelling and prophecy as foretelling, since very frequently God's future mode of action, on account of Israel's or her oppressor's sin, is foreshadowed. It is impossible to declare the will and purpose and judgment of God without reference to the future. The prophets threaten, and every threat involves the future. They may be distinguished as prophets of weal or of woe, and both of these terms imply the future." Any Bible reader is familiar with the frequent New Testament claim, "that it might be fulfilled"; a claim which is essentially true if we allow for what someone has called "an element of novelty" in the fulfillment, and for what A. G. Hebert in *The Throne of David* calls "the central theme of the Bible": the Messianic hope. There is prediction in the prophecy of the Old Testament; but there is also *teaching,* and this too is reflected widely and deeply in the New Testament. In a book of mine called *Prophecy Interpreted* I point out that there are *three* "Time-Dimensions" of prophecy: past, present, and future. It is rooted in the Covenant which God made with his people in the past, and in the Torah which God gave to guide his people in the good and the right way of his will. It addressed itself to the continuing historical situation, with a message alternately of judgment or of salvation. Because of the promise involved in the covenant at the beginning it looked forward into the distant future with the hope of ultimate fulfillment of God's purpose in choosing a people to be "his very own," a people with a mission that concerned the world. Illustrations both of preaching and of prediction as a part of the prophetic message will follow. At the moment let it suffice to stress the fact that prophecy consists of both; and which of the two is the more important it is hard to say. The best approach is to recognize the presence and the significance of both.

How Was the True Prophet Accredited?

If there were false prophets as well as true who sought the ear of the chosen people it becomes a matter of some importance to distinguish between the two. How was a true prophet accredited and recognized in Israel?

The classic passage concerning the accreditation of the prophet as a Teacher is found in Deuteronomy 18: 15-22. The true prophet followed in the footsteps of Moses, and his preaching and teaching was in fundamental conformity with that of the Torah which was the fundamental law of the land. This was true of the whole Old Testament prophetic institution as well as of the prophetic ministry of Christ, and of those disciples of Christ who possessed in a special sense the gift of prophecy. *The Westminster Dictionary of the Bible* sums it up in these words: "Every prophet of God, and preeminently Christ, was like unto Moses (Deuteronomy 18: 18; Acts 3: 22, 23), in similarity of enduement, of doctrine, of attitude towards the Law, of didactic work." This does not mean that they were all monotonously the same in their teaching, but the element of fundamental unity is there. Even the Law and the Gospel, though different, are not contradictory of each other. The true prophet shared every concept in our Hebrew-Christian heritage that we have discussed: they all preached in accordance with the religion of Israel.

We need not repeat what the content of this heritage was: we need only reemphasize one significant point in it, its teaching concerning Yahweh as the LORD God of Israel. In Deuteronomy 13: 1-5 there is a significant warning against the false prophet, and it involves just this test of *true theology.* Even if a self-professed prophet should be able to perform signs and wonders, and even if some of his predictions for the future should come to pass, yet if he urged the people of Israel to forsake the living God for other gods they must not listen to him: "for the LORD your God is testing you, to know whether you love the LORD your God with all your heart and with all your soul." There is a sternness to Deuteronomy 13: 5 that is sobering in the extreme: "But that prophet or that dreamer of dreams shall be put to death, because he has taught rebellion against the LORD your God, who brought you out of the land of Egypt and redeemed you out of the house of bondage, to make you leave the way in which the LORD your God commanded you to walk. So you shall purge the evil from the midst of you."

It is true that the Old Testament prophet was at times accredited also by signs and wonders, just as the New Testament preacher; but miracles were only a secondary form of accreditation. The performance of miracles could add weight to a prophet's credentials *if* they were accompanied by conformity to the word of God previously given to his people but never if the prophet's teaching contradicted that word of God. The strong ethical character of the prophet's preaching also served as a part of his credentials. So also did the overwhelming conviction of many of the prophets that they were chosen, prepared, and called of God. The call was often soul-searching in nature, as in the case of Moses, Samuel, Jeremiah, and Ezekiel. It was reenforced by the repeated statement that "the word of the Lord came." The prophet Amos has expressed this conviction perhaps as clearly and forcefully as anyone in chapter 3: 7-8:

> "Surely the Lord God does nothing
>   without revealing his secret
>   to his servants the prophets.
> The lion has roared;
>   who will not fear?
> The Lord God has spoken;
>   who can but prophesy?"

The prophet Jeremiah has expressed it in more personal terms in chapter 20:9,

> "If I say, 'I will not mention him,
>   or speak any more in his name,'
> there is in my heart as it were a burning fire
>   shut up in my bones,
> and I am weary with holding it in,
>   and I cannot."

Coupled with this overwhelming conviction there was a willingness on the part of many of the prophets to suffer persecution as a result of their faithfulness in proclaiming the word of God for their own day. All of these things continue to speak to us as credentials for these men whose message is such an important part of our Hebrew-Christian heritage.

What then about the predictive element of prophecy? Here too the true prophet had impressive credentials to offer in the form of *fulfillment of their prophecy*. This fulfillment had a twofold character. There was first fulfillment in what we might call a short-range sense, applying especially to prophecies of judgment which were often fulfilled within the life-time of the prophet or in the near future. It is true that there were also "conditional" prophecies, where the prophetic word led to repentance and repentance became the occasion for God to change the threatened judgment into deliverance. Every prophecy must be studied in the light of its purpose and also of its historical results. But as "prophets of doom" the true prophets of Yahweh had the gift of seeing "in which direction" events were flowing and to gift of sight they added that of courage to proclaim what they saw, even when it made them extremely unpopular in their own generation. But they were also prophets of hope, because they were assured that all the promises of God from Abraham on were faithful and true. Therefore while the old covenant seemed to be collapsing they preached of a new covenant; or of a renewal and reaffirmation and fulfillment of all that for which the covenant with Israel as God's "very own" stood as the original type and representative. Some of these prophecies of hope were fulfilled before the Old Testament ended; in the main, however, we look to the New Testament, where we have the prophetic word made more sure, for the final confirmation and fulfillment of God's covenant purpose. It is here that we look for the fulfillment of "the Messianic Hope" in the broad sense in which A. G. Hebert speaks of it in the *The Throne of David*. It is here that we find the fulfillment of the promise and commission to Abraham, of which the present author has spoken at length in *God's Covenant of Blessing*. We shall devote one whole chapter to the relation between the Two Testaments, noting among other things "the element of novelty" in the New, which makes it a fulfillment and yet something more than a simple repetition of the Old. Yet, from the prophetic point of view, there remains an essential unity both of preaching and of prediction in the scriptures on which our Hebrew-Christian heritage is based.

Who Were the Prophets?

There were many prophets in Israel. On at least one occasion Abraham is called a prophet. So is Moses, who at one time appeared before the people of Israel with seventy elders who prophesied (Numbers 11); and when two who remained in camp also prophesied and were criticised for it, Moses answered them with the wish, "Would that all the Lord's people were prophets, that the Lord would put his spirit upon them!" (Numbers 11: 29). Samuel is sometimes called "the father of prophecy;" and his significance for the development of the ethical nature of the writing prophets was certainly great as was also his position as head of "the company of the prophets": and yet he was not alone. He was undeniably "the earliest of the great Hebrew prophets after Moses": a teaching and a judging prophet, whose relation to the kingship resembled that of many of his successors. There were other non-writing prophets of renown, such as Elijah and Elisha and Nathan and Gad and Micaiah: to each of whom was committed a definite mission from the Lord. The so called "writing prophets" began to appear near the middle of the 8th century B.C. and continued for more than four centuries. Four of them belonged to the 8th century B.C.: Amos, Hosea, Isaiah of Jerusalem, and Micah. They were essentially preaching prophets, in whose message the ethical note is strong; but not to the exclusion of the religious relationship to God. They belonged to the Assyrian world situation, and the note of impending judgment on Israel because of her sins shows clearly the direction in which events were flowing. At the same time there is a pronounced teaching element which is reflected in the New Testament and is a vital part of our Hebrew-Christian heritage.

There were also four writing prophets in the 7th century B.C.: Nahum, Zephaniah, Jeremiah, and Habakkuk. The world situation had changed from that of Assyrian to Chaldean or Babylonian dominance, and the prophets reflect the change; although in their preaching they do not differ greatly from their 8th century predecessors. The note of judgment on Israel is still the same; and there is the same profound spiritual and ethical content. The relevance of these prophecies for their own historical situation must not be overlooked. Only then will we be able to apply what is permanent in them to our own situation today; that is, to understand in what sense they belong to our Hebrew-Christian heritage.

Two prophets belonged to the 6th century B.C. Ezekiel prophesied both before and during the Babylonian Exile, with the judgment motif to the fore in the first half of the book and the hope motif in the second part. The author of Isaiah 40-66 probably lived during the latter part of the Exile, when the hope of an imminent return from captivity burned brightly; and there is no other part of the Old Testament wherein the theme of redemption, or the Messianic Hope, is as prominent as here. Even so we must bear in mind that these hope prophecies combine the promise of a coming restoration from the Babylonian Captivity with the promise of a redemptive experience which went far beyond the history of Israel, and by injecting that element of novelty of which we have spoken before connect the Old Testament hope with the New Testament fulfillment. It is obvious that the study of prophecy involves a complex as well as significant insight into our Hebrew-Christian heritage. We can in the course of this brief chapter touch on only a few of the highlights of the phenomenon that we know as Hebrew or Old Testament prophecy; and what we are trying to do right now is to see these prophets in their historical perspective and succession.

After the return of a remnant of Israel from the Babylonian Captivity we note three prophets whom we may properly call "post-exilic." They are Haggai, Zechariah, and Malachi. Some of the problems they faced were entirely different from those that confronted earlier prophets. The same may be said of the three prophets that are undated: Joel, Jonah, and Obadiah. Here we may draw some cautious conclusions as to date and authorship from the contents of the prophecies; but we do best if we simply listen to the message and try to see what there is in it for us.

The Message of the Prophets

Perhaps the same can be said about *all* the writing prophets, whose ministry in Israel covered a span of some five centuries. What *is* the word of the Lord which came to them, and continues to come to us as we read them today? The answer can only be a brief summary of the most significant concepts, unless we choose to write a commentary on them all. But some things can be said with assurance as well as for edification.

1. There are some books with a very distinctive theme, which gives unity to the whole. We list a few of them by way of illustration.

The Book of Amos has been aptly characterized by J. E. McFadyen as "A Cry for Justice."

The Book of Hosea has an overall theme which might well be phrased as "The Love of God for His Wayward People."

The Book of Nahum is a prophecy concerning "The Overthrow of Nineveh."

The theme of the Book of Zephaniah is "The Day of the Wrath of the Lord."

The Book of Jonah has a missionary motif: "God's Concern for Heathen Nineveh."

The Book of Habakkuk is a prophetic study in "The Problem of Theodicy."

On the other hand, the larger books such as Isaiah, Jeremiah, and Exekiel, and even some of the shorter ones such as Micah, contain a wide selection of prophecies, each a unit in itself, on widely divergent themes. For example, Isaiah 5: 1-7, "The Parable of the Vineyard," is such a unit. So is Isaiah 40, which is one of the greatest chapters in the Old Testament, and in which we can still discern "The Lord's Comforting Words to his People," whether we think of that people as Israel or as the Christian Church. Another outstanding chapter is Jeremiah 7, with its plea to "Amend Your Ways and Your Doings." Other passages will be listed as we make a topical approach to the message of the prophets.

2. One of the commonest aspects of the prophetic message is the indictment of God's people for their sinfulness in relation to the covenant requirements and to the covenant God. In a sense this is the negative side of the Torah or the Law; or shall we say that it is the application of the principles of the Torah to the present historical situation, which was often marked by apostasy. We shall list a few striking examples, which serve to express God's judgment on a wrong relationship whether to God or to fellow-men: violations of both the first and the second great summarizing commandments on which the life of God's people was established by the moral law of Yahweh, the ethical heart of our Hebrew-Christian heritage.

Amos, whose message has been called "A Cry for Justice," has several outstanding passages of the kind just described. For example, chapter 2: 6-8, which we quote:

> Thus says the LORD:
> "For three transgressions of Israel,
>   and for four, I will not revoke the punishment;
> because they sell the righteous for silver,
>   and the needy for a pair of shoes —
> they that trample the head of the poor into the dust of the earth,
>   and turn aside the way of the afflicted;
> a man and his father go in to the same maiden,
>   so that my holy name is profaned;
> they lay themselves down beside every altar
>   upon garments taken in pledge;
> and in the house of their God they drink
>   the wine of those who have been fined."

We grant that such sins from ancient days may need interpretation in terms of our own days; yet even the casual reader cannot fail to get the impression of oppression and affliction and uncleanness and carousing and the violation of the laws both of justice and mercy. The same is true of the passage in chapter 5: 10-13, which is followed by the double admonition to "Seek good, and not evil" and to "Hate evil, and love good." An even more remarkable passage is found in Amos 8: 4-7 which the reader is strongly urged to read because of the vividness with which it describes oppression, injustice, and greed, and the boldness with which it declares God's judgment upon it.

One of the clearest passages of this type is found in Isaiah 5: 1-7, in the Parable of the Vineyard. We quote only the interpretation in verse seven:

> "For the vineyard of the LORD of hosts
>   is the house of Israel,
> and the men of Judah
>   are his pleasant planting;
> and he looked for justice,
>   but behold, bloodshed;
> for righteousness,
>   but behold, a cry!"

From verse eight on there follows a series of six Woes pronounced on the Wicked. The sins are many, but both here and elsewhere in Isaiah they can be classified as sins of apostasy or of oppression and injustice; that is, they are sins against both God and our neighbor. Some prophets such as Hosea emphasize the sin of apostasy; others, like Micah, put greater stress on injustice. There is no stronger denunciation of injustice in all literature, secular or spiritual, than in Micah 3: 1-4:

> "And I said:
> Hear, you heads of Jacob
>   and rulers of the house of Israel!
> Is it not for you to know justice? —
>   you who hate the good and love the evil
> who tear the skin from off my people,
>   and their flesh from off their bones;
> who eat the flesh of my people,
>   and flay their skin from off them,
> and break their bones in pieces,
>   and chop them up like meat in a kettle,
>   like flesh in a caldron.
> Then they will cry to the LORD,
>   but he will not answer them;
> he will hide his face from them at that time,
>   because they have made their deeds evil."

But an equally vivid denunciation of apostasy is found in Jeremiah 2:
12-13:

> "Be appalled, O heavens, at this,
>   be shocked, be utterly desolate, says the LORD,
> for my people have committed two evils:
>   they have forsaken me,
> the fountain of living waters,
>   and hewed out cisterns for themselves,
> broken cisterns,
>   that can hold no water."

Jeremiah 7: 8-11 combines the sin against man with that of a false worship of God: "Behold, you trust in deceptive words to no avail. Will you
steal, murder, commit adultery, swear falsely, burn incense to Baal, and
go after other gods that you have not known, and then come and stand
before me in this house, which is called by my name, and say, 'We are
delivered!' — only to go on doing all these abominations? Has this house,
which is called by my name, become a den of robbers in your eyes? Behold, I myself have seen it, says the LORD."

The prophets are full of such denunciations as these, of which we can
give only a few illustrations. What the prophets exposed was *a wrong
relationship* to God and man: a persistent transgression of the first and
the second great commandment, which made a mockery of their calling to
be "a people of God." Their preaching was aimed first at achieving
repentence if possible, and then at pronouncing judgment in historical
terms if there was no repentance. The same thing is true of our Hebrew-
Christian heritage which reflects the message of the prophets.

3. However, what we may call the positive preaching side of the Law
is not ignored in Hebrew prophecy. It may be true that the prophets spent
more time denouncing sin than they did in proclaiming righteousness;
and yet the two are closely interwoven. Sometimes the emphasis is on the
divine Teaching as to what is good and right and true, as well as on the
divine promises of grace and mercy whenever God's people return to him
in penitence and obedience. In Isaiah 30: 21 we are told, "And your ears
shall hear a word behind you, saying, 'This is the way, walk in it,' when
you turn to the right or when you turn to the left." If we ask, What was
this way?, there are clear answers, of which we cite only a few. In Isaiah
1: 16-17 the admonition both as to repentance and as to righteousness is
clear:

> "Wash yourselves; make yourselves clean;
>   remove the evil of your doings
>   from before my eyes;
> cease to do evil,
>   learn to do good;
> seek justice,
>   correct oppression;
> defend the fatherless,
>   plead for the widow."

In Isaiah 32: 14-18 there is a beautiful description of the future prospect of God's people when justice and righteousness will dominate the scene because "the Spirit is poured upon us from on high"; and the result of righteousness will be peace, and quietness, and trust, for ever. This was the glorious hope that God held before the eyes even of his sinful people, because it expressed what God wanted for them and what he wanted them to be.

Among the great teaching passages in the prophets we shall mention only a few. For example:

Hosea 6: 6
> "For I desire steadfast love and not sacrifice,
>   the knowledge of God, rather than burnt offerings."

Amos 5: 24
> "But let justice roll down like waters,
>   and righteousness like an everflowing stream."

Micah 6: 8
> "He has showed you, O man, what is good;
>   and what does the LORD require of you
> but to do justice, and to love kindness,
>   and to walk humbly with your God?"

Isaiah 1: 18-20
> "Come now, let us reason together,
>   says the LORD:
> though your sins are like scarlet,
>   they shall be as white as snow;
> though they are red like crimson,
>   they shall become like wool.
> If you are willing and obedient,
>   you shall eat the good of the land;
> But if you refuse and rebel,
>   you shall be devoured by the sword;
>   for the mouth of the LORD has spoken."

Isaiah 40: 10, 11

"Behold, the Lord God comes with might,
    and his arm rules for him;
behold, his reward is with him,
    and his recompense before him.
He will feed his flock like a shepherd,
    he will gather the lambs in his arms,
he will carry them in his bosom,
    and gently lead those that are with young."

Isaiah 57: 15

"For thus says the high and lofty One
    who inhabits eternity, whose name is Holy:
'I dwell in the high and holy place,
    and also with him who is of a contrite and humble spirit,
to revive the spirit of the humble,
    and to revive the heart of the contrite.' "

Jeremiah 6: 16

"Thus says the LORD:
'Stand by the roads, and look,
    and ask for the ancient paths,
where the good way is; and walk in it,
    and find rest for your souls.'
But they said, 'We will not walk in it.' "

Jeremiah 22: 15-16

"Do you think you are a king
    because you compete in cedar?
Did not your father eat and drink
    and do justice and righteousness?
    Then it was well with him.
He judged the cause of the poor and needy;
    then it was well.
Is not this to know me?
    says the LORD."

Ezekiel 11: 19-20

"And I will give them one heart, and put a new spirit within them; I will take the stony heart out of their flesh and give them a heart of flesh, that they may walk in my statutes and keep my ordinances and obey them; and they shall be my people, and I will be their God."

Ezekiel 18: 23

"Have I any pleasure in the death of the wicked, says the LORD God, and not rather that he should turn from his way and live?"

Habakkuk 2: 4

> "Behold, he whose soul is not upright in him shall fail,
> but the righteous shall live by his faith."

Malachi 3: 6

> "For I the LORD do not change; therefore, you O sons of Jacob,
> are not consumed."

We could continue almost indefinitely with such teaching gems from the prophets, which are also a part of our Hebrew-Christian heritage; but let us sum up by noting that they center around such great religious and moral truths as justice, righteousness, peace, steadfast love, the knowledge of God, obedience and faith, a right relation to the will of God for our manner of life, both in relation to God himself and to our neighbor. Trust in the LORD, and do good, is the fundamental teaching of both prophecy and psalmody, as well as of the Torah. It is also the fundamental teaching of our Hebrew-Christian heritage.

4. Another frequent theme in Hebrew prophecy is the denunciation of a purely formalistic ritual worship devoid of ethical content. Piety, which is a form of worship, is no substitute for ethics, which is a way of life. Of course, the reverse is also true. Ethics as a way of life is no substitute for true piety in worship. The two belong together. We list a few of the more significant prophetic passages where religion without ethical conduct is sharply criticized. We suggest that the reader look them up and study them carefully.

Isaiah 1: 10-17
Jeremiah 7: 1-23
Hosea 6: 1-6
Amos 5: 21-24
Micah 6: 1-8
Isaiah 66: 1-4

Sacrificial worship was a part of Israel's religion, and it has something to teach us still by way of symbolism; but worship went deeper than that: it involved a true knowledge of God, a genuine recognition of the God of the covenant in spirit and in truth, and with this recognition a humble submission to his will in relation to our neighbor. We seem to come back to this simple fact stated by Jesus that both the law and the prophets are based upon the twin commandments of love to the Lord our God and of love for our neighbor as ourselves. There can be no worship of him in spirit and in truth without them.

5. We have spoken of the prophetic denunciation of sin; but with this denunciation two accompanying prophetic notes are sounded.

The one is the call to repentance, of which Isaiah 31: 6 is a vivid illustration: "Turn to him from whom you have deeply revolted, O people of Israel." Often this plea for repentance was in vain, as when we read in Jeremiah 8: 4-7 of Israel's turning away "in perpetual backsliding," when "no man repents of his wickedness" but instead "refuse to return." The earnest plea in Ezekiel 18: 30 is typical of all the prophets: "Repent and turn from all your transgressions, lest iniquity be your ruin." The pathos of the situation is reflected by the refrain in Amos 4: 6-11, "yet you did not return to me, says the Lord." The intenseness of the divine yearning for the return of his sinful people can be seen in Joel 2: 12-14:

> " 'Yet even now,' says the LORD,
>   'return to me with all your heart,
> with fasting, with weeping, and with mourning;
>   and rend your hearts and not your garments.'
> Return to the LORD your God,
>   for he is gracious and merciful,
> slow to anger, and abounding in steadfast love,
>   and repents of evil.
> Who knows whether he will not turn and repent,
>   and leave a blessing behind him,
> a cereal offering and a drink offering
>   for the LORD, your God?"

If there is such repentance there is a sure promise of restoration: "You will seek me and find me; when you seek me with all your heart, I will be found by you, says the LORD, and I will restore your fortunes and gather you from all the nations and all the places where I have driven you, says the LORD, and I will bring you back to the place from which I sent you into exile." (Jeremiah 29: 13, 14). But where there is no repentance the prediction of judgment is swift and sure. In the Old Testament it usually took the form of an historical calamity such as exile, which would take place in the near future. The eighth century prophets predicted the Assyrian Captivity, and the prediction was fulfilled. In Amos 6: 14 we hear of an oppressor-nation, as yet unnamed, but doubtless Assyria; in Hosea 9: 3 we read of a new captivity in Egypt and Assyria; in Isaiah 10:5-11 Assyria is referred to as "the rod of my anger;" in Micah 1:2-16 the Assyrian invasion is described as by an onlooker, who may have lived in Moresheth-gath (vs. 14). The seventh century prophets predicted the Babylonian or Chaldean exile, and again the prediction was fulfilled. This is true of Habakkuk, Jeremiah, and Zephaniah, as well as of Ezekiel whose ministry extended into the exile itself. But because of God's faithfulness to his covenant the last word cannot be judgment or captivity, or even discipline. The prophets were convinced of an eventual consummation of God's covenant with his people, and they foretold it in various ways: without setting forth a detailed time-chart or chronological schedule of times and seasons. Just as God made the covenant in the first place, so he will find a way of bringing it to its eventual consummation. The Old Testament prophets speak much of a new or revitalized covenant, of a return or restoration to the land of promise, of a remnant, of a restored Davidic kingdom. Some of this has the same immediacy as the judgment predictions; this is true especially of the prophets living within the period of the exile, such as the latter half of Ezekiel's ministry, as well as the ministry of the socalled Second Isaiah. But there is a marked difference in emphasis on repentance and judgment, sin and restoration, in the Old Testament as compared with the New. In the Old Testament the perspective is laregly national: the entire covenant people is concerned. In the New Testament the viewpoint is more markedly personal; as when John writes in I John 1: 6-9, "If we say we have fellowship with him while we walk in darkness, we lie and do not live according to the truth; but if we walk in the light, as he is in the light, we have fellowship with one another, and the blood of Jesus his Son cleanses us from all sin. If we say we have no sin, we deceive ourselves, and the truth is not in us. If we confess our sins, he is faithful and just, and will forgive our sins and cleanse us from all unrighteousness." Speaking on the same personal level the apostle Paul says in Romans 6: 23, "For the wages of sin is death, but the free gift of God is eternal life in Christ Jesus our Lord." Contrast the two words: *exile* and *death*, and you see the difference between the Teaching of the Old Testament and the New concerning the judgment for sin. Yet both are a part of our Hebrew-Christian heritage.

6. Something must be said about the Messianic overtones to Old Testament prophecy; for it is at this point that the New Testament interpretation becomes so significant. We cannot go into detail. Suffice it to say that there are several outstanding themes as well as chapters that merit close study as a part of our Hebrew-Christian heritage. One is connected with the Davidic kingship, and the hope of a restored kingdom of David. Franz Delitzsch once called Isaiah 7-12 "the Book of Immanuel"; and within this section we find three significant prophecies that relate to the future fulfillment of the Davidic kingship. There are others;

for example, in Micah 5: 2-5; in Jeremiah 23: 5-6; and in Ezekiel 21: 25-27. There is also the concept of the Servant of the Lord, so prominent in Isaiah 40-55, and related in Acts 3: 26 to "my servant Jesus." The future coming of God himself, with mercy and with might, as set forth in Isaiah 40: 10-11, is Messianically significant. So is the concept of Yahweh as the good shepherd of his sheep in Ezekiel 34. The covenant relationship between Yahweh and Israel is a type of the new covenant which came into being through Jesus Christ. It is not always easy to see the Messianic significance as we read the Old Testament prophets. There are two reasons for this. One is hinted at in I Peter 1: 10-11, when the apostle says that the prophets were not always fully aware of the spiritual depths of their own message: they like we continually "searched and inquired about this salvation" of which they prophesied by the word of the Lord which came to them. The other is explained by F. N. Jasper when he says that there is in the fulfillment of prophecy "an element of novelty." Nevertheless, in their overall proclamation of the word concerning God, Man, Sin, Judgment, and Salvation, as well as concerning the coming of God himself into the historical situation, their message remained fundamentally Messianic or Messianically oriented; and so does our Hebrew-Christian heritage.

7. It should not be overlooked that while the prophetic message concerned especially Israel as the people of God in their continuing relation to God's will it did assume authority to pronounce judgment on other nations as well. These were, of course, nations that belonged to what we call the biblical world: that were related historically in some sense to Israel. The effect of these prophecies is to show Yahweh, the God of Israel, as the Lord of the nations. We find collections of such prophecies in Amos 1-2, in Isaiah 13-23, in Jeremiah 46-51, in Ezekiel 25-32, in the book of Nahum. More rarely we find a message of promise and hope for the nations, as if to spell out the promise to Abraham that he and his descendants would be a blessing to all the nations of the world. The book of Jonah contains such a missionary theme. Even more remarkable is the prophecy in Isaiah 19: 24-25, where two of Israel's ancient enemies are spoken of not only in terms of receiving but of being a blessing. Let me quote the passage: "In that day Israel will be the third with Egypt and Assyria, a blessing in the midst of the earth, whom the LORD of hosts has blessed, saying, 'Blessed be Egypt my people, and Assyria the work of my hands, and Israel my heritage.'" Here we are practically on New Testament ground in its assertion of the universality of the gospel and

of God's redeeming love. Of such stuff is our Hebrew-Christian heritage made.

8. In conclusion we would simply call attention to the changing prophetic treatment of a single concept or subject. By way of example we select the prophetic treatment of Assyria and its capital Nineveh. We could just as well have chosen the theme of the servant of the Lord. But with respect to Assyria-Nineveh we find at least five different points of view: 1) in Isaiah 10: 5-11 Assyria is called "the rod of my anger," God's instrument of judgment upon Israel; 2) in Hosea 9:3 and 10:6, and context, Assyria is the place of a new captivity like that which Israel had once experienced in Egypt; 3) in Nahum the prophet predicts judgment upon Nineveh and its eventual overthrow; 4) in Jonah Nineveh is the object of God's pity and compassion, of his saving love; 5) in Isaiah 19: 24-25, which we have already quoted Assyria shares the calling of Israel to be a blessing in the midst of the earth. What is needed here is obviously a theological rather than a strictly literal interpretation with an emphasis on typology. Only extensive readings in the prophets, following some of the guidelines indicated in this chapter, will show the extent to which it has become a part of our Hebrew-Christian heritage. The two main guidelines, of course, are the *preaching* and the *prediction* of the prophets, their dual role as *forthtellers* and as *foretellers* of the word of the Lord which came to them, and which through them comes also to us.

Chapter 8

THE CONCEPT OF HISTORY

Our study now will move to the concept of history in our Hebrew-Christian heritage. Our primary emphasis will be on the *teleological* character of the Hebrew concept of history; but there are some other significant aspects that deserve consideration before we get to teleology.

History and Prophecy

There is a close association between history and prophecy in Hebrew thought and teaching. We have already seen something of this association in our study of prophecy. What we say now will therefore be partly repetitious, but it should also serve to clarify the association.

For example, the arrangement of books in the Hebrew Old Testament is both interesting and significant at this point. Where the English Bible arranges the material in 39 books, the Hebrew Bible arranges substantially the same material in 24 books, grouped in three sections. First is the Torah, or the five books which we associate with the name of Moses and call the Pentateuch. The second division is called the prophets and includes eight books: four of these are called the *former* prophets and four the *latter* prophets. The former prophets are the books which we usually call *historical*: Joshua, Judges, I and II Samuel as one book, and I and II Kings as one book. We shall return to them in a moment. The latter prophets are what we call the *writing* prophets: Isaiah, Jeremiah, Ezekiel, and the Twelve Minor Prophets as one book. The remaining eleven books of the Old Testament are called simply *the writings*. Of the 24 books Genesis stands first and Chronicles last; so that where we refer to the whole Old Testament after this manner, "from Genesis to Malachi," the Hebrew would say "from Genesis to Chronicles." Incidentally, this sheds light on Matthew 23: 35, with its reference to two Old Testament martyrs, one in Genesis and one in Chronicles; suggesting the whole sweep of martyrdom from beginning to end. But we return as promised to the former prophets, which we call the historical books of the Old Testament. The Hebrew arrangement and nomenclature clearly suggest the concept of history written from a prophetic point of view. The Hebrew "historian" makes no claim that his work represents a purely objective history, in the sense of a recital of facts and nothing more: he points to the revelation of God in the events of history and couples with that revelation the prophetic interpretation of its real significance.

The same emphasis on prophetic interpretation is found in the frequent references to historical sources that lie behind the books in their present form. For example, in I Chronicles 29: 29-30 we read: "Now the acts of King David, from first to last, are written in the Chronicles of Samuel the seer, and in the Chronicles of Nathan the prophet, and in the Chronicles of Gad the seer, with accounts of all his rule and his might and of the circumstances that came upon him and upon Israel, and upon all the kingdoms of the countries." Here the names of three outstanding prophets of Israel are associated with the keeping of historical accounts if not with the actual writing of history. In II Chronicles 32: 32 we read: "Now the rest of the acts of Hezekiah and his good deeds, behold, they are written in the vision of Isaiah the prophet the son of Amoz, in the Book of the kings of Judah and Israel." There is a similar reference to Isaiah and history writing in connection with the reign of Uzziah. The conclusion from the evidence at hand would seem to be that the prophets were both chroniclers and interpreters of the chief events in the history of the chosen people.

The close association between prophecy and history is also confirmed by the active participation of many prophets in the events of Israel's history. That is especially true of the earlier non-writing prophets, such as Samuel in the 10th century B.C., and of Elijah and Elisha in the 9th century. The prophet Nathan occupied a position which might be called that of "court chaplain" to David; and in this role he advised him not only religiously but politically. Both Isaiah and Jeremiah were actively involved in the history of their times. In their prediction of judgment, whether on Israel or on the surrounding nations, almost all of the prophets were concerned with politics as well as with religion; and that means that their messages became a cross-section of current history. In short, prophecy and history belong together in the Old Testament; and this relationship is reflected in our Hebrew-Christian heritage.

Yahweh as the Lord of Israel's History

The biblical faith in Yahweh as the Lord of Israel's history is consistent throughout. We see it from the call of Abraham on. We see it in the events of the Exodus which led to the formation of Israel as the covenant people of God. We see it in the five great "faith-events" to which G. Ernest Wright has called our attention in *The Book of the Acts of God*. A good sample statement is found in Exodus 6: 6-8, which we have quoted elsewhere: the predictive summary of the deliverance from the land of Egypt and the steps leading to the formation of the covenant and the wilderness journey which brought them finally into the land of promise. One of the clearest statements about "the God who acts in history" is found in Micah 6: 3-5, which is worth quoting:

> "O my people, what have I done to you?
> In what way have I wearied you? Answer me!
> For I brought you up from the land of Egypt,
> and redeemed you from the house of bondage;
> and I sent before you Moses,
> Aaron, and Miriam.
> O my people, remember what Balak king of Moab devised,
> and what Balaam the son of Beor answered him,
> and what happened from Shittim to Gilgal,
> that you may know the saving acts of the LORD."

A similar historical summary is found in Amos 2: 9-11. Countless illustrations could be added to show that Yahweh was regarded as the Lord of Israel's history. Israel was the chosen people of Yahweh. Their history began, and continued, and would ultimately conclude according to the dictates of the covenant of Yahweh with them. According to our Hebrew-Christian heritage the same is true of the history of the New Testament people of God; that is, of the Christian Church.

Yahweh the Lord of the Nations

But according to biblical history, and according to the teaching of our Hebrew-Christian heritage, the Lord of Israel's history was also the Lord of the nations surrounding Israel, and in a sense involved in the history of Israel. These were the nations of the Mediterranean world, which is sometimes called the biblical world. We need not repeat from the chapter on prophecy the listing of the chapters in Amos, Isaiah, Jeremiah, Ezekiel, and Nahum that pronounce judgment upon some of these nations. It might make the picture more vivid if we enumerate them: from Amos, Damascus, Gaza, Ashdod, Tyre, Edom, Ammon, and Moab; from Nahum, Assyria; from Isaiah, Babylon, Philistia, Moab, Damascus, Ethiopia, Egypt, and Tyre; from Jeremiah, Egypt, the Philistines, Moab, Ammon, Edom, Damascus, and Babylon; from Ezekiel, Ammon, Moab, Edom, the

Philistines, Tyre, Sidon, and Egypt. Two impressions stand out: first, that Yahweh is Lord not only over his people Israel but also over their enemies: that both are responsible to the judgment of his just and holy will; and second, that the nations mentioned are such as were in close geographical and historical relationship to Israel. There is no attempt to enumerate all the nations on the face of the earth, although the principle of Lordship over Israel's contemporaries would seem to apply with equal validity on a worldwide scale. The Lord rules over all, and we see this rule especially in the exercise of judgment in the historical situation of the moment.

It is not only *in his judgment* upon the nations, however, that the universal lordship of Yahweh is asserted. In Isaiah 10: 5-11 Assyria is seen as the instrument of God in the discipline of his "godless" people: Assyria is "the rod of my anger, the staff of my fury," which the LORD uses for his judgment against Jerusalem and Samaria. Yet, when the king of Assyria ascribes this victory to his own strength and wisdom instead of recognizing in it the hand of the LORD, the prophet quickly and vividly puts this arrogance in its proper historical perspective:

> Shall the ax vaunt itself over him who hews with it,
> or the saw magnify itself against him who wields it?
> As if a rod should wield him who lifts it,
> or as if a staff should lift him who is not wood! (Isaiah 10:15)

The LORD *uses* Assyria and other heathen nations in the discipline even of his own chosen people, but it is *the LORD alone who rules*. The same note is sounded in Habakkuk 1: 6 with respect to the Chaldeans, "For lo, I am rousing the Chaldeans": for the purpose of punishing evil in Judah. In Jeremiah 27: 6, in the same historical context, Yahweh calls Nebuchadnezzar, the king of Babylon, "my servant"; for from the prophetic point of view he served Yahweh in bringing about the Babylonian Captivity. In Isaiah 45: 1, in another historical context, Cyrus is referred to as the Lord's anointed, to whom was given the commission of bringing about Israel's release from captivity. In Amos 9: 7 we find a surprising prophetic statement which seems to put Israel on the same level as the Philistines and the Syrians:

> "Are you not like the Ethiopians to me,
> O people of Israel?' says the LORD.
> 'Did I not bring up Israel from the land of Egypt,
> and the Philistines from Caphtor and the Syrians from Kir?' "

What is asserted here is Yahweh's sovereignty over all nations; it does not nullify the uniqueness of his covenant purpose with Israel. Through

Abraham they had been called to be a blessing in the midst of the earth. They could fulfill their calling only by being obedient to the will of Yahweh their God and by walking in his ways: that is, by acknowledging his Lordship. In the chapter on prophecy, however, we learned from the marvelous prophecy in Isaiah 19: 24-25 that Israel's ancient enemies, Egypt and Assyria, were called to share with Israel both in receiving and in being a blessing: and this too could only come to pass as the Gentiles or the nations acknowledged with Israel what it means that Yahweh is LORD. Already here in our Hebrew-Christian heritage we find a preview in the Old Testament of a teaching that dominates the New: a universality which can be summed up in the words of Obadiah 21, "the kingdom shall be the Lord's." The assertion of the principle that God rules the nations is a fundamental part of our Hebrew-Christian heritage. Just how God exercises this rule over the world of nations is admittedly often a mystery. Sometimes faith can see and recognize the act of God in history only after the event. This is especially true when he acts in judgment. There is a moral law which is operative in history even when it seems to be ignored. Perhaps all that we can say with the certainty of conviction is that God has the last word when wickedness runs rampant: his judgments in history are for real! But there is more to it than that in Hebrew-Christian thought, where the fundamental assumption is that God is in control of history, both in the punishment of evil and in the achievement of good.

The Teleological Concept of History

What we have said thus far has led up to what we want to say now about the teleological concept of history. Perhaps the word *teleological* is not familiar to you. Perhaps it is not the best word for what we have in mind. Perhaps *eschatological* would be a better term to use. But I do not think so.

Teleological suggests to me the idea of *purpose* and *goal*, which are inseparable from the Hebrew concept of history. As Claude Tresmontant points out in *A Study of Hebrew Thought,* it runs counter to the Greek cyclical concept of history: history seems to be an endlessly repetitious circle which gets nowhere. It also runs counter to the current view of the meaninglessness of history. It asserts that history has a goal which has been set by God, and that it will some day reach that goal. This is especially true of the biblical concept of history as it centers in the history of God's people; but this religious history is seen very clearly as a part of world history, which also is forward moving and looks forward in spite of many aberrations to a goal.

1. We began to see this teleological concept of history when we were considering the concept of creation. We recall Edmond Jacob's characterization of creation as having "a commencement," "a sequel or a continuation (which has the character of history)," and finally also an end. That is, creation is eschatological in character (Ludwig Koehler); and to say that it is eschatological means much the same thing as to say that it is teleological. There is a purpose with creation; it has meaning; it moves onward towards a goal.

2. What we have said about creation is equally true about the covenant. We might venture to say that it is more clearly so in the case of the covenant. Consider, for example, the call of Abraham: both the commission to "be a blessing" and the promise that "in you and in your seed all the families of the earth will be blessed." The Covenant of Blessing with Abraham dominates both Old Testament and New Testament history. When in the Old Testament it seemed as if the apostasy of Israel might bring the covenant to nought we find it significantly reaffirmed in the promise of "the new covenant" in Jeremiah 31: 31-34. Read it carefully. It does not really matter if we call it a reaffirmation or a revitalization of the old; for it is true that if you think simply in terms of the concepts involved there is nothing really new here. The law of God written in their hearts; the relationship of "their God — my people"; the universal knowledge of God; the forgiveness of sins: all of these can be shown to have been inherent in God's intention with the original covenant with Israel. What is new is that the prophecy visualizes *an experimental consummation* of what was incipient in the old: the covenant becomes what it was meant to be, its purpose becomes actual reality. This is the teleological hope of the Old Testament. The New Testament makes it clearer still by way of fulfillment in Christ and in his people the Church. In the deepest sense, when our Hebrew-Christian heritage thinks of history it thinks of Old Testament prophecy with a New Testament fulfillment. It thinks in terms of teleology, or of a firm Old Testament hope, not always clearly spelled out, and leaving room for "an element of novelty" in the fulfillment: but always looking forward to a divinely set goal. In a sense that goal was reached in "the new covenant in Jesus' blood;" in another sense it is still partly unfulfilled: but *fulfillment* belongs to the ultimate goal, because history is teleological, it is not meaningless, it has a goal. We need no clearer statement of that goal than the one we find in the promise to Abraham, "in you all the families of the earth will be blessed." It is in the light of that covenant promise that our Hebrew-Christian her-

itage understands the history of Israel, and ultimately the coming of Jesus Christ in whom we have been blessed "with every spiritual blessing in the heavenly places," as well as the history of the Christian Church whose mission is to proclaim this blessing until Jesus comes again to complete it all.

3. We shall give only a few additional illustrations of this teleological concept of biblical history, which is shared by our Hebrew-Christian heritage. These illustrations are not necessarily synchronized as to time, so as to form a uniform picture of the end times or the last things. The prophets, and we are dependent largely upon them for the Hebrew interpretation of history, differ both in language and in perspective, and they employ a variety of symbols; but they are united in their concept of a God who acts in history, and therefore of a divine purpose being worked out in history, and most important of all, of a goal which will ultimately be reached.

For example, in Isaiah 65: 17-25 there is a significant prophecy linking together history and creation: God will eventually create "new heavens and a new earth," and this new creation will mark the consummation of his activity in history. How will this new creation be characterized, according to the prophet? Chiefly by peace and security: the absence of the sound of weeping and of the cry of distress. Another way to express it is to say that the ideal relationship between God and his people will be realized; the hindrances to the full outpouring of God's blessings will be removed; there will be joy for weeping, and length of days, and peace as in a paradise restored. The New Testament, in II Peter 3: 13, picks up the prophecy and adds to it the "element of novelty," when it says: "But according to his promise we wait for new heavens and a new earth in which righteousness dwells." There will come a day when righteousness and peace will prevail. Such is God's goal. Such is his promise. Such is the hope which constitutes the teleological character of the concept of history in our Hebrew-Christian heritage.

And speaking of peace on earth as the teleological goal of history we must not overlook the prophecy in Micah 4: 1-5, with its almost verbatim parallel in Isaiah 2: 2-5. Look it up and read it carefully. What a vision of hope it holds before our eyes! We urged that it be read with care because it speaks of peace in a far different and deeper sense than much of the visionary talk of our day. The basis for this future peace is the recognition by "many nations" of the preeminence of the religion of Yahweh and the willingness of the nations to be taught the ways of God and to walk in them. There can be no permanent peace among men without first establishing a right relationship with God. Only as men seek and submit to the living God, the Holy One of Israel, and submit their lives to the guidance of his word, can there be peace. When men submit to God's judgment, peace will follow. On that basis only can there be lasting peace on earth. What we have here in Micah and in Isaiah is a glorious prophecy of hope which runs counter to all outward appearances in the world of men. It is a hope shared by many, by all who really accept our Hebrew-Christian heritage. The only question is as to time: will that day come soon? We dare to believe that it will come because God has said so: it is his goal for mankind.

Another frequent teleological note in biblical history is that of the restoration of a remnant of Israel from captivity, and of the raising up of the fallen Davidic kingship. A good example is to be found in Amos 9: 11-15. A complete exegesis in terms of Israel's history is not possible here. Suffice it to say that the language is in part symbolic and in part historical. There was a partial fulfillment of the prophecy in the history of Israel. According to Acts 15: 15-17 there is an element of Messianic hope in the first part of the prophecy, which found fulfillment in the coming of Jesus Christ. Following up this spiritual interpretation we might say that it is being fulfilled now through the Christian Church as it exalts the lordship of kingship of Jesus Christ. But whether we stress the hyperbolic language referring to Israel's renewal, with its blessings of prosperity and peace, or put the emphasis on the Messianic implied in the restoration of the house of David, the one significant aspect of the prophecy is that it obviously looks forward to a goal: it is teleological in character.

The same can be said of the frequent references to "the day of the Lord" as a day of final judgment. It can be said of the prophecy in Ezekiel 40-48, with its vision of the restored temple. A literal interpretation here leads us into endless contradictions; but this truth stands out clearly, "The reality will correspond to the divine ideal." The divine ideal first expressed in terms of the tabernacle, and then of the temple, will become reality: the purpose of God will be realized as history reaches its goal. Let us repeat, for it bears frequent repeating, that there will be *an element of novelty* in the fulfillment; but the very fact of fulfillment, in whatever form, is teleological. God acts in history to achieve his goal.

In terms of the individual this truth is beautifully formulated in Psalm 16. Read it with care. It gives the impression of faith in a fellowship with God which goes all the way, in life, in death, and beyond. The teaching of the psalm is akin to Romans 8: 38-39 which affirms that there is no separation from the love of God which is in Christ Jesus our Lord. *Nothing* can stop God from achieving the goal of his purpose with his creation. If in no other way, it will be as we read in Revelation 21: 5, "And he who sat upon the throne said, 'Behold, I make all things new.'" In Acts 3: 18-21 we read of "the time for establishing all that God spoke by the mouth of his holy prophets from of old." James Moffat's translation makes this even clearer, "till the period of *the great Restoration.*" What it all signifies is that history moves towards a goal: it is a part of God's ongoing purpose, and however dismal the prospect at times, it will not fail to reach that goal. Therefore we live in hope, as the prophets did; as Paul did and urges us to do: "May the God of hope fill you with all joy and peace in believing, so that by the power of the Holy Spirit you may abound in hope." See Romans 15: 13.

A Summary

Claude Tresmontant has summed up the teleological nature of the Hebrew concept of history in *A Study of Hebrew Thought*:

"History is not an eternal flow of unrelated events. It has a beginning (bereschit), and is ordered to an end, just as the tree's growth is ordered to fruitfulness. — It is characteristic of biblical history that those who carry it forward are made aware of its *direction* through the teachings of the prophets. The prophet, the *nabi,* is someone who understands the 'sense' of history, what it means and whither it moves. — A historical event is a *sign* only in so far as one may read in it what will come of it, just as we can foretell, when the bud appears, that the flower will follow. It is not because of some extrinsic relationship, but very simply because the former actually does produce the latter. The *nabi* is aware of God's creative action and understands those 'phases' of it which regard man especially."

History is teleological because there is a living God who acts with purpose to achieve a goal. This is the faith of our Hebrew-Christian heritage.

Chapter 9

THE CONCEPT OF PSALMODY

One of the most influential Old Testament books as touching our Hebrew-Christian heritage is the Psalter or the Book of Psalms. It can be classified both as a Hymn Book and as a Book of Prayer and Praise. It grew out of, and in turn nurtured, the life of worship in Israel; and it has had a profound influence upon Christian worship as well. G. Ernest Wright is probably correct when he says in *The Book of the Acts of God* that "the Book of Psalms has been the most widely read book in the Old Testament." It has been the subject of much scholarly study; but we shall attempt a more simple approach, which will enable us to see some of the ways in which a devout Christian can make use of the Psalms today, both in community and in private worship. But first a brief introduction to the history of psalmody in Israel, and a clear distinction between the function of psalmody and prophecy.

The Psalter as a Hymn Book

According to the *Westminster Dictionary of the Bible* the Hebrew book of Psalms was "the hymn book of the Second Temple," the one built after the return from the Babylonia Captivity. That is undoubtedly true; but there are indications that some of the Psalms, perhaps even most of them, were in existence *before* the Exile, and may have been used in the worship in Solomon's Temple or earlier.

In the last line of II Samuel 23: 1 David is called "the sweet psalmist of Israel." Another possible translation makes David "the favorite of the songs of Israel." The one translation links him with the authorship and the other with the theme of the Psalms. There is probably a measure of truth in both. Hans Wilhelm Hertzberg, in his *Commentary on the Book of Samuel,* makes this comment about II Samuel 23: 1-7: "Today an increasing body of opinion, in accordance with tradition, regards David as the author of the poem from at least vs. 3b onwards; there are hardly any decisive arguments to be brought against this position." We know, of course, that the titles of almost half of the Psalms ascribe their authorship to David; and while this tradition may not be decisive, it does confirm the statement by Hertzberg which definitely links sacred music with the name of David. This statement by G. Ernest Wright is significant: "Liturgical music and psalmody, therefore, owe their origin in Israel to David. This should not be interpreted to mean that David wrote all the music himself, nor that he composed the psalms which were used as the text to be sung. It means rather that he was the patron of religious music." In another place he says, "The psalms represent every phase of Israelite life between at least the tenth century B.C. and the time of Nehemiah and Ezra."

John Wm. Wevers may be quite right when he says in *The Way of Righteousness* that "no one knows who wrote the psalms." He adds, however, that "this does not mean that David wrote no psalms; it means that no one knows whether he did." With such statements we have no quarrel; for the question of authorship is not fundamental to a right use of the psalms in our own devotional life. We are happy to add, however, a statement by Helmer Ringgren in *Faith of the Psalmists*: "Together with a growing number of Old Testament scholars we shall assume that most of the psalms are pre-exilic" and that they reflect for the most part "the official pre-exilic religion of Israel." It is as such that they have great significance for our Hebrew-Christian heritage.

More significant than the references to authorship in the psalm titles are the musical notations, which confirm that they were sung to the accompaniment of stringed instruments. The exact meaning of each musical notation is uncertain, but the presence of such notations is not. This tends to confirm the assertion of Helmer Ringgren that "the religion of the Psalms is cultic religion. The Psalms were not written for private use — at least not originally — but for use in the cult of the Yahwistic community, and in most cases for the cult of the pre-exilic community." Artur Weiser, as we shall see later, conceives of the milieu out of which the Psalms come as an annual covenant renewal festival. The only modification that we would make of each of these statements is that a psalm may well have been composed by an individual for private use and then adopted by the cultic community for use in public worship. Some of the psalms are too personal in character to suppose that they were composed by or in a group; and group authorship is in its very nature a procedure too vague to imagine. The title to Psalm 102, "A prayer of one afflicted, when he is faint and pours out his complaint before the Lord," presupposes the lamentation of an individual, which is taken up by the congregation because it represents a common experience.

But laying questions of authorship aside, we shall concern ourselves more with the contents or the words, as we do with our Christian Hymnals: and that leads us to the Christian use of the Psalms as a Book of Prayer and Praise. We shall note other classifications too; as Wevers does, when he classifies the Psalms as Psalms of Complaint, of Confession, of Thanksgiving, of Trust, of Dedication, of Intercession, and of Adoration. Our own grouping will be slightly different: we shall look at the Book of Psalms as a Book of Prayer, as the Book of Praises, as a Confession of Faith, as a Confession of Sin and Need, as Teaching in the Good and the Right Way, as Meditations on the Will and Works of God, as Curse Psalms directed against Evil, and as Covenant Renewal Psalms. We may add a section of Royal or Messianic Psalms. How does each fit into our private and public worship; what does each contribute to our Hebrew-Christian heritage?

A BOOK OF PRAYER

The Psalter among other things is a book of Prayer. As we well know, prayer is an essential element in all true Christian worship; and a knowledge and use of the Psalter may help us to find words with which to pray, as well as to receive inspiration for prayer. We can only illustrate briefly, of course. There is a note of petition or of prayer, together with other facets of worship, in almost every psalm; but there are some prayers that are exceptionally beautiful and significant and relevant to the Christian life.

For example:

1. There is first of all what I love to call "the prayer for a listening ear." How important that is in prayer! It is beautifully illustrated in Psalm 4: 1.

> "Answer me when I call, O God of my right!
> Thou hast given me room when I was in distress.
> Be gracious to me, and hear my prayer."

It is frequent in the Psalms. Lord, hear me, listen to me, answer me, be gracious and merciful to me: let me know that you are near, that you care, that you are a prayer-answering God! Prayer could stop right there and be meaningful.

2. Then there is the prayer of one in great need or suffering, when God seems far away. This is a not uncommon experience in life. We find a

good example of it in Psalm 13, which opens with a fourfold cry of "How long?" "How long, O Lord? Wilt thou forget me for ever?" Then in verses 3 and 4 comes the prayer:

"Consider and answer me, O Lord my God;
    lighten my eyes, lest I sleep the sleep of death;
lest my enemy say, 'I have prevailed over him;'
    lest my foes rejoice because I am shaken."

What does such a petition mean? It is a plea to be saved, from suffering, from affliction, from imminent death; from "my foes." Perhaps the psalmist was thinking of actual enemies which surrounded him and endangered his life; it is easy, and legitimate, to spiritualize these enemies as Luther does, so that the prayer becomes essentially a prayer for deliverance from sin, death, and the power of the devil. What the psalmist needed, and what we need, is the assurance that God has not forsaken him, that in every time of affliction of whatever sort he is safe in the presence of God. In verse 5 he expresses his confident faith in God's steadfast love. In verse 6 he sings his praise. A Christian can pray like that for help in every time of need.

3. There is a significant prayer in Psalm 19: 12-14, as a conclusion to the Meditation on the Works and Word of God. We might truthfully say that the Meditation led to prayer, as it usually does. There are three petitions. The first is this: "clear thou me from hidden faults." It follows the confession, "But who can discern his errors?" It amounts to this: clear me from the sins of which I am not even aware! How important it is to make that confession, and to pray that prayer; for it is not an easy thing for a man to know himself so well that there is no secret sin in his heart or in his life. God knows us better than we know ourselves, and only he can clear us from error and secret or unintentional sins. The second petition is this: "Keep back thy servant also from presumptuous sins; let them not have dominion over me!" This prayer has to do with the sins *of which I am aware,* and which threaten to gain control over me; it is a prayer for strength to resist, a prayer for help to refrain from willful sins. It is in this context that the psalmist makes bold to say: "Then shall I be blameless, and innocent of great transgression." There is such a thing as prayer that leads to victory over besetting sins, if not to complete sinlessness. The third petition is the wellknown and oft-quoted petition in verse 14:

"Let the words of my mouth and the meditation of my heart
    be acceptable in thy sight,
    O LORD, my rock and my redeemer."

In short, keep my words and my thoughts always such as to be pleasing in the sight of God. Surely a Christian can and should pray like that; or to put it differently, such should be the fervent hope and ardent prayer of his heart always.

4. There are many prayers in Psalm 25, but the most suggestive passage for the Christian prayer life is found in verses 4-7. Look it up and read it carefully. It is a prayer for guidance in "the good and the right way," to use the words of the prophet Samuel in I Samuel 12: 23: that is, in God's way, as he has made it clear for us in his Word. It is a prayer to be led in the way of truth: that is, in God's truth and in the constant experience of his faithfulness. It is a prayer for God to be continually mindful of his grace and mercy towards us: that is, of his steadfast love. (The Hebrew word *hesed,* which RSV translates as 'steadfast love,' is probably the most beautiful word in the Old Testament.) It is a prayer that our former, youthful sins may be forgotten, and, of course, forgiven. If we continue on into verse 11 we find a prayer also for forgiveness of all present sin and guilt, however great it may be. Surely a Christian can and should pray like that! He can make the very words his own as a part of our Hebrew-Christian heritage.

5. Just in passing let us notice the unique prayer in Psalm 56: 8. "Thou hast kept count of my tossings; put thou my tears in thy bottle! Are they not in thy book?" We remember how Jesus said that the very hairs of our head are all numbered by our heavenly Father. The psalmist says that God keeps track of every tear that we shed. It is a prayer of assurance that God is concerned about our every need. The Christian needs to pray with such assurance; and according to our Hebrew-Christian heritage he has the right to do so.

6. We shall look at Psalm 119 from another point of view than that of prayer a little later; but it is interesting to note that in a didactic psalm like this there are more than 50 verbs of petition, some of which are used several times.

7. There are two significant prayers in Psalm 143. The first is in verses 1 and 2; the second is in verses 7-10. Each is worth quoting in full, with explanatory comments.

> "Hear my prayer, O LORD;
>   give ear to my supplications!
> In thy faithfulness answer me,
>   in thy righteousness!
> Enter not into judgment with thy servant;
>   for no man living is righteous before thee."

This is the familiar prayer for "a listening ear:" hear and answer me. On what basis does the psalmist presume to make this request? On the basis of mercy, not of merit. Because of God's faithfulness and righteousness. Because he has promised to hear and answer prayer. Then the petition becomes more specific: do not judge or condemn me. I am sinful. No man can pretend to be otherwise and get by with it. But God is faithful and righteous to forgive when we ask for it sincerely. The line of thought is the same as in I John 1: 9.

In verses 7-10 (perhaps especially in verses 8 and 10) we have one of the most beautiful and wonderful morning prayers ever composed and prayed by man. We suggest that you read the whole passage, but we shall quote verses 8 and 10 before commenting on the whole.

> "Let me hear in the morning of thy steadfast love,
>   for in thee I put my trust.
> Teach me the way I should go,
>   for to thee I lift up my soul.
> Teach me to do thy will,
>   for thou art my God!
> Let thy good spirit lead me
>   on a level path!"

Looking at the prayer as a whole we note requests such as these: Make haste to help me! Do not turn away from me. Let me hear anew each morning of thy steadfast love: that is, let me experience it again every day. Teach me the right way: show me what it is. Deliver me from my foes who would hinder me from walking in that way. Teach me not only to know but to do thy will: that is, help me to walk in the way which has been revealed to me as the good and the right way. Lead me by thy Spirit on a level path: that is, in a safe and secure way. Do this today! Do this every day! What a marvelous prayer! Can we possibly improve on it as a morning prayer, any more than we can improve on the Lord's Prayer? It is a part of our Hebrew-Christian heritage to pray like that. The challenge is to try it and to experience that it works.

8. There are a number of psalms that are almost pure petition from beginning to end. Some of them are called "A Prayer" in the title. We shall mention a few — and return to some of them in another connection. For example:

Psalm 51 begins with what we call the chief petition, the petition which covers every need, whether it be spiritual or material: Have mercy on me, be merciful to me. In this psalm it is a prayer for forgiveness and cleansing. There are nineteen verbs of petition which are essentially variations on the same theme. Most familiar among them is the petition, "Create in me a clean heart, O God." Since it is a penitential psalm we shall consider it again, and more in detail, when we look at this category of psalms.

Psalm 86 is called "A Prayer of David." There are fifteen verbs of petition: for a listening ear; for answer to prayer; for preservation and deliverance in time of need; for grace, mercy, and pity; for a true knowledge of God's way; for strength and salvation. The most unique petition in the psalm is found in the last line of verse 11:

> "Teach me thy way, O Lord,
>   that I may walk in thy truth;
>   unite my heart to fear thy name."

This is a prayer for wholehearted devotion to God, not only in worship, but in walking in the way of his truth.

Psalm 90 is called "A Prayer of Moses, the man of God." Authorship does not concern us, but the contents of the psalm does. The viewpoint is that of the transcience of life, which leads to dependence on the living God. The most significant petition is found in verse 12:

> "So teach us to number our days
>   that we may get a heart of wisdom."

Psalm 17 is also called "A Prayer of David." Among its many familiar petitions there is one that is uniquely beautiful. We find it in verse seven.

> "Wondrously show thy steadfast love,
>   O savior of those who seek refuge
>   from their adversaries at thy right hand."

9. Since the use of the psalms is "a learning experience" in prayer, we must not overlook *the condition* for God's answer to prayer. That he was a prayer-answering God the faith of the psalmists took for granted. So does our Hebrew-Christian heritage. But in Psalm 66: 16-20 we learn that God does not hear and answer every prayer, regardless of the state of heart of the man who prays. It is not an impossible condition, for the man who wrote these verses claimed to have met the condition and to have received the answer. We quote the passage in full:

"Come and hear, all you who fear God,
        and I will tell what he has done for me.
I cried aloud to him,
        and he was extolled with my tongue.
If I had cherished iniquity in my heart,
        the Lord would not have listened.
But truly God has listened;
        he has given heed to the voice of my prayer.
Blessed be God,
        because he has not rejected my prayer
        or removed his steadfast love from me!"

Two things stand out as "conditions" for answered prayer: the one is God's steadfast love; the other is the fact that there is no attempt on man's part to excuse or to "cherish" sin. The confession of sin and need must be honest; the desire to be forgiven and cleansed and kept in the will of God must be sincere. If this condition be met the prayer will not be rejected, says the writer of this psalm. He had tried it and he knew that whoever comes in the right spirit can depend on the steadfast love of God to both hear and answer prayer.

10. In summary: all that we have tried to do is to give a little glimpse of what the Book of Psalms can mean as "a Book of Prayer" for the Christian's life of prayer. It can act as an incentive to pray; and it can help us with the very words to use in prayer: it can provide us with "prayers to pray." If it had no other role to play in our Hebrew-Christian heritage it would still be a precious book. But there is more to come!

THE BOOK OF PRAISES

In the Hebrew Bible the title of the Book of Psalms is *sepher tehillim*, which means "the Book of Praises." It is a good title, although some find fault with it because not all psalms are praise psalms. In fact, Psalm 72: 20 seems rather to stress the prayer element which we have been discussing. Nevertheless many psalms are pure praise, and most psalms, even the psalms of lamentation, contain some element of praise. It is certainly a significant element in the Psalter.

If prayer is essential to Christian worship and helpful in the Christian way of life, so also is praise and thanksgiving. There can be no strong spiritual life without a thankful heart nor can there be a complete worship without a song of praise. The New Testament makes that clear in Colossians 3: 16-17. So also does the Old Testament Psalter, for example in Psalm 147: 1.

> "Praise the LORD!
> For it is good to sing praises to our God;
> > for he is gracious, and a song of praise is seemly."

There is, of course, a slight difference between thanksgiving and praise, though we use the terms here as if they were almost interchangeable. We thank God for what he has given or for what he has done; we praise him for what he is. But it is through what he gives and does that we learn to know his character or his nature as our God.

But why should we praise him? For what should we give thanks? Again we must resort to illustrations of how the psalmist thought and spoke and learn from him.

1. The parallelism between thanksgiving and praise is illustrated in Psalm 30: 4 —

> "Sing praises to the LORD, O you his saints,
> > and give thanks to his holy name."

2. The admonition to give thanks, and some of the many reasons for giving thanks, is illustrated in Psalm 136, a liturgical praise psalm, which begins with the thrice-repeated admonition:

> "O give thanks to the LORD, for he is good,
> > for his steadfast love endures for ever."

The only variation in the three verses is in the fact that the admonition is to give thanks to the LORD, then to the God of gods, and finally to the Lord of lords. The psalm closes on the same note:

> "O give thanks to the God of heaven,
> > for his steadfast love endures for ever."

3. Psalm 145 is called "A Song of Praise," which it certainly is. God is praised for his greatness and for his goodness, for his majesty and for his compassionate mercy. The whole creation, and especially the whole family of man, is urged to give praise to God. It is from this psalm that we have the familiar table prayer which is so definitely a part of our Hebrew-Christian heritage:

> "The eyes of all look to thee,
> > and thou givest them their food in due season.
> Thou openest thy hand,
> > thou satisfiest the desire of every living thing."

Of course there is a problem connected with the promise: the problem of poverty, which is so largely man-made but which to the unthinking person may seem to give the lie to the word of God. Perhaps the promise was easier to believe, and the praise therefore came more readily, when the human population was limited, and the food supply sufficient. But it can be true even today if man will cooperate with God and not waste his resources so freely given. Jesus spoke in the spirit of this psalm when he said in the Sermon on the Mount: "Therefore do not be anxious, saying, 'What shall we eat?' or 'What shall we drink?' or 'What shall we wear?' For the Gentiles seek all these things; and your heavenly Father knows that you need them all. But seek first his kingdom and his righteousness, and all these things shall be yours as well." (Matthew 6: 31-33). This is the language of faith, directed especially to the people of God who recognize him as the Giver of every perfect gift, and who are willing to acknowledge their duty to share what they have received with others. Most of all it is a confession of faith which praises God for what he is:

"The LORD is gracious and merciful,
    slow to anger and abounding in steadfast love.
The LORD is good to all,
    and his compassion is over all that he has made."

(Psalm 145: 8-9)

4. Another and more familiar song of praise is Psalm 103. The verb *bless* is used here as the equivalent of *praise*, adore, give thanks. Note carefully the list of "benefits" listed in verses 2-5, for which the psalmist urges himself to bless the LORD. They are such major gifts as forgiveness, spiritual and physical health, deliverance from premature death, the experience of steadfast love and mercy, and in general the satisfaction "with good" as long as life lasts. After the recital of these personal benefits he tells about God's wonderful works and way in relation to his people Israel, which we may rightly apply also to the Christian Church, and in a limited sense, even to our nation. Included in the list are justice, grace and mercy, steadfast love, forgiveness, compassionate pity on man as a creature of dust and yet a child of God, the covenant bond between the LORD and his people. This is no "grocery list" approach to God, and yet all of life is encompassed: all the things that really count in life are included. Bless the LORD, O my soul!

5. Psalms 104 and 105 also begin with self-exhortation, "Bless the LORD, O my soul." In Psalm 104 God is remembered for his manifold works in creation and also in providence. We note especially verses 27-30:

125

"These all look to thee,
　to give them their food in due season.
When thou givest to them, they gather it up;
　when thou openest thy hand, they are filled with good things.
When thou hidest thy face, they are dismayed;
　when thou takest away their breath they die
　and return to their dust.
When thou sendest forth thy Spirit, they are created;
　and thou renewest the face of the ground."

In Psalm 105 God is praised for his wonderful works in history, especially in the history of Israel. The reference to his covenant with his people in verses 7-11 is one of the most beautiful in the Old Testament:

"He is the LORD our God;
　his judgments are in all the earth.
He is mindful of his covenant for ever,
　of the word that he commanded, for a thousand generations,
the covenant which he made with Abraham,
　his sworn promise to Isaac,
which he confirmed to Jacob as a statute,
　to Israel as an everlasting covenant,
saying, 'To you I will give the land of Canaan
　as your portion for an inheritance.' "

6. A frequent verb of admonition in Hebrew is the word Hallelujah, which in translation means "Praise ye the Lord." We have taken it into the English language as an expression, a veritable shout, of praise. One section in the Psalter, from 113 to 118, has sometimes been called the Great Hallel, because of the prominence in it of this word as well as of the whole concept of praise. It was commonly sung at the Passover celebration, and may well have been the hymn mentioned in Matthew 26: 30, which Jesus sang together with his disciples just before they went out to the Mount of Olives. If you will read the closing verses of Psalm 118 you can relive in imagination a most moving event. It was with words of thanksgiving upon his lips that Jesus went out to Gethsemane and Golgotha, to suffer and die for us all: "Thou art my God, and I will give thanks to thee; thou art my God, I will extol thee. O give thanks to the LORD, for he is good; for his steadfast love endures for ever!" What an example for us, who so often complain when life is difficult: forgetting not only the example of which Paul speaks in Philippians 2: 5-8, but also the admonition of Peter, in I Peter 4: 19, "Therefore let those who suffer according to God's will do right and entrust their souls to a faithful creator." The Psalter as a part of our Hebrew-Christian heritage can teach us to give thanks *always* and *in everything*.

7. This becomes even clearer in what I for one like to call the Hallelujah Chorus of the Book of Psalms: the closing section, in Psalms 146-150. In every psalm we find the familiar Hallelujah, "Praise the LORD!" Psalm 146 begins with the promise, "I will praise the LORD as long as I live; I will sing praises to my God while I have being." Psalm 147: 1 tells us why: "For it is good to sing praises to our God; for he is gracious, and a song of praise is seemly." Psalm 149: 1 urges us to "Sing to the LORD a new song, his praise in the assembly of the faithful." In each of the five psalms there are abundant reasons given for praising God, rising to a mighty climax in Psalm 150: which ends on this all-inclusive triumphant note of praise: "Let everything that breathes praise the LORD! Praise the LORD!" It reminds us of Wennerberg's great Cantata based on Psalm 150, which rises to a crashing crescendo of praise; but it reminds us also of the many praise hymns in every Christian hymnal. For praise as well as prayer is a fundamental component of our Hebrew-Christian heritage: it was a fundamental part of worship in the Old Testament, and it is so also in the New Testament and in the Christian Church.

A CONFESSION OF FAITH

We turn to another element in our Hebrew-Christian heritage based on the Psalter which overlaps the first three: it is almost throughout a confession of faith. All true worship is an act of faith. There can be no prayer nor praise without faith. The very names used for God in the Psalms are indicative of a basic faith. It is as when *we* say, taught by the Lord Jesus, "Our Father who art in heaven": we are in essence saying to God, "This is what we believe that you are in relation to us." We use other terms of address also, of course; and rightfully so, for we grope for words to express fully the wonders of God's Being and of his relationship to Man. The psalmist did the same thing; though one of the commonest terms of address was Yahweh, the LORD, which we have earlier refined as "Self-manifesting existence." Gerhard von Rad, in his little book *"Moses,"* calls attention to the fact that in Old Testament faith "the *Name* of God and *His saving will* are inseparably held together." Certainly that is true of the name Yahweh, the LORD, the personal name of the God of Israel. A good introduction to the life of prayer even for the Christian is the proclamation of "the name of the LORD" in Exodus 34: 5-8. Read it! God is like that, and when we pray we pray to a God like that. It is a part of our Hebrew-Christian heritage.

We are especially interested right now, however, with the Confession of Faith which characterizes certain psalms or portions of psalms.

1. There is first the familiar, beautiful, and beloved Psalm 23. "The LORD is my shepherd," says the psalmist; anticipating the New Testament statement by Jesus, "I am the good shepherd." Because of this shepherd-role of God three things are true: I shall not want, but enjoy abundant provision for every need; I will fear no evil, but enjoy the protection of his presence even in the valley of the shadow of death; I shall dwell in the house of the LORD for ever, and enjoy his perpetual and eternal goodness and mercy. What more can we ask?

2. Almost as wonderful a confession of faith is found in Psalm 27. This psalm has precious memories for me from my Confirmation Day, when my mother gave it to me as "a word for the day." Verse one tells what God is to me:

> "The LORD is my light and my salvation;
>   whom shall I fear?
> The LORD is the stronghold of my life;
>   of whom shall I be afraid?"

In verses 2 and 3 we hear of what God does for me. In verse 4 we have a statement of the "one thing" that I seek from the LORD: to dwell in his house, in worship and adoration, now and forever. There follows in verses 5-6 the assurance that he will make me secure in the day of trouble, and the promise to sing his praise in faith and joy. The actual prayer of faith follows in verses 7-12: here the confession of faith is, as it were, crystallized. It is worth reading over and over again. The psalm concludes with an exhortation to continue in faith:

> "Wait for the LORD;
>   be strong, and let your heart take courage;
>   yea, wait for the LORD!"

Can we find better words with which to express a living faith and to pray for our actual needs in life?

3. Another great psalm of faith is Psalm 16. The theme is found in verses one and two: "Thou art my LORD; I have no good apart from thee." Tracing this theme through the psalm, sometimes in the language of imagery as in verses 5 and 6, sometimes as the assertion of a present experience as in verses 7 and 8, we reach the triumphant conclusion of faith in verses 9-11:

"Therefore my heart is glad, and my soul rejoices,
　　my body also dwells secure.
For thou dost not give me up to Sheol,
　　or let thy godly one see the Pit.
Thou dost show me the path of life;
　　in thy presence there is fullness of joy,
　　in thy right hand are pleasures for evermore."

What the psalmist confesses in faith is a life with God that just cannot end! There is a strong resemblance to Psalm 23: 4, where the psalmist confesses that he is unafraid even when walking through the valley of the shadow of death: "for thou art with me." Franz Delitzsch calls it a confession of faith in eternal life which is not yet formulated as a doctrine but can best be called "a leap or portulate of faith" based on experience. The New Testament counterpart is Romans 8: 37-39. It is a part of our Hebrew-Christian heritage that there is nothing, neither life nor death, which can separate us from the love and presence of God. The psalmist saw it dimly, whereas we see it now in the light of the resurrection of Jesus Christ.

4. There are two great confessions of faith with respect to the forgiveness of sins, in Psalms 32: 1-5 and 130: 1-4. At these we shall look later in another connection. Let us look right now at Psalm 139, which is one of the most doctrinal of the psalms, and as such is also a psalm of faith. Someone has expressed its theme in these formidable theological words: "the Omniscient and Omnipresent Omnipotence of God." What it means is simply this: God knows all about me, as one who has searched and known my thoughts, words, and ways (verses 1-6); God is everywhere present, which gives the believer a wonderful sense of security and guidance and care (verses 7-12); God is the almighty Creator, who has also made me (verses 13-16), so that I am not only dependent upon him for everything but assured that he cares for me. If one may "rate" psalms as "great" or "greater," this is certainly one of the "greatest"; and it is a part of our Hebrew-Christian heritage. The closing prayer in verses 19-24 deserves careful consideration, both with respect to "the wicked" and "any wicked way" and with respect to God as our guide in the way everlasting. God searches the heart and tests both thought and action: faith submits to his leading in the right way.

5. A favorite prayer of faith is Psalm 121. Will you take time to read it? Two words stand out: "help" and "keep." To the man who wrote this psalm God was the One from whom help came when it was needed. He

was the One who kept the psalmist's life from all evil. He can be the same to us.

> "The LORD will keep
> your going out and your coming in
> from this time for evermore."

Such is the faith of our Hebrew-Christian heritage.

6. There are many other psalms which contain an element of confession of faith. We cannot mention them all. We conclude this section by referring the reader to Psalm 46, on which Martin Luther based his great hymn, "A Mighty Fortress is our God."

The Penitential Psalms

In the tradition and use of the Christian Church seven psalms came to be known as the "Seven Penitential Psalms." They are Psalms 6, 32, 38, 51, 102, 130, and 143. Since these are so definitely a part of our Hebrew-Christian heritage we must take note of them; although honesty compels us to admit that the penitential element is equally strong in some other psalms, and that it requires careful exegesis to find it in some of the "Seven Penitential Psalms." Psalm 6 is one of these. It is certainly a "Prayer for Mercy in Time of Trouble," as the heading in RSV indicates; but the trouble is just as certainly in part of a physical nature. Since this is not a commentary we let it go at this that it is probably psycho-somatic in character: that is, both physical and spiritual, with the one affecting the other.

Psalm 32 speaks first of all about the blessedness or happiness of the one whose transgression is forgiven and whose sin is covered; and then, by way of contrast, it describes the unhappy state of him who refuses to confess his sin, and to ask and to receive forgiveness. In both instances the writer speaks from personal experience.

From Psalm 38 we quote only this striking confession:

> "I confess my iniquity,
> I am sorry for my sin."

This is what we mean by penitence; and it is the first step to forgiveness.

Psalm 51 is throughout a prayer for mercy, cleansing, forgiveness. It evinces a deep consciousness of sin as separating the sinner from God. One of its more familiar verses is the prayer that God would "create in me a clean heart," and that he would put within me "a new and right spirit." The psalmist is equally concerned that God would not reject him: that is, that he would not cast him away from his presence or take his holy Spirit from him. With the assurance of a favorable answer to his prayer he promises to teach other transgressors God's ways, especially how to return to him when they have strayed into a life of sin, and for his own personal deliverance he promises to sing aloud to God with songs of thanksgiving.

Psalm 102 we shall consider in another connection. According to the title it is "A prayer of one afflicted, when he is faint and pours out his complaint before the LORD." As in Psalm 6 we must look for an association between the experience of affliction and the consciousness of sin. They are in actual fact often related, though not necessarily so.

It is in Psalm 130 that we find the suppliant sinner crying out from the depths to the LORD and then confidently asserting his faith in a God who forgives. We quote the first four verses:

"Out of the depths I cry to thee, O LORD!
    Lord, hear my voice!
Let thy ears be attentive
    to the voice of my supplications!
If thou, O LORD, shouldst mark iniquities,
    Lord, who could stand?
But there is forgiveness with thee
    that thou mayest be feared."

The last two lines remind us of Psalm 86:5, "For thou, O Lord, art good and forgiving, abounding in steadfast love to all who call on thee." Instead of the adjective "forgiving," according to W. O. E. Oesterley, the Hebrew would permit translation as "a forgiver": that is, it belongs to the very nature of God to forgive sins.

The last of the penitential psalms is Psalm 143. The penitential element is confined to the first two verses, which we quote, with special emphasis on the sweeping assertion in the last line:

"Hear my prayer, O LORD;
    give ear to my supplications!
In thy faithfulness answer me,
    in thy righteousness!
Enter not into judgment with thy servant;
    for no man living is righteous before thee."

It is this sweeping assertion of universal sinfulness which characterizes our Hebrew-Christian heritage. There was only one exception: Jesus Christ.

The Teaching Aspect of the Psalms

There is a teaching element interwoven with prayer and praise, and with the confession of faith and of sin, in the Psalter. For example, there is the teaching in Psalm 23 that "the LORD is my shepherd," with all that this relationship involves for my life. There is the teaching in Psalm 139 that God is Omniscient, Omnipresent, and Omnipotent. There is the teaching in Psalm 145 that God is great, and God is good. There is the teaching in Psalm 27 that "the LORD is my light and my salvation." And so we could continue with practically every psalm that we have so far considered.

But there are also purely didactic psalms, with a more direct teaching character, and we want to look also at a few of these as a part of our Hebrew-Christian heritage.

For example, Psalm 1 gives us an insight into the Old Testament believer's view of the Law that should not be foreign to the New Testament believer. Notice the attitude of the psalmist in verses 1-3 and how it affected his life:

> "Blessed is the man
>   who walks not in the counsel of the wicked,
> nor stands in the ways of sinners,
>   nor sits in the seat of scoffers;
> but his delight is in the law of the LORD,
>   and on his law he meditates day and night.
> He is like a tree
>   planted by streams of water,
> that yields its fruit in its season,
>   and its leaf does not wither.
> In all that he does, he prospers."

The first part of Psalm 19 is a meditation on "The Works and Word of God" (RSV), in which we learn to know him in the glory of his creation and in the perfection of his Torah or Law. The same theme is found on an enlarged scale in Psalm 119. The "quotes" at the top of pages 643-648 in RSV show us how this teaching is mingled with ardent prayer. The prayer to "teach me" is frequent in the Psalter: usually as a prayer to be taught the ways of God and how to walk in them. See, for example, Psalm 25: 4-5 and Psalm 143: 8, 10.

There are also historical psalms such as Psalm 104, which recites the wonderful creative works of the LORD, still continuing; Psalm 105, which is an historical recital of God's covenant faithfulness to Israel; and

Psalm 106, in which we are told of the repeated rebelliousness of Israel against the LORD. In Psalm 37, especially in verses 1-9, there is an almost prophetic exhortation, which is summed up in the line, "Trust in the LORD, and do good." The same prophetic character of the psalm is illustrated in the key-verse (verse 9):

"For the wicked shall be cut off;
    but those who wait for the LORD shall possess the land."

This prophetic teaching concerning God's judgment on the wicked and blessing on those who seek earnestly to walk in his ways continues throughout the long exposition that follows.

We need not elaborate further. The point is that the teaching element, while not the primary function of the Psalter, is still an important part of our Hebrew-Christian heritage. There is both law and prophecy in the Book of Psalms. According to the New Testament interpretation some of the prophetic passages are Messianic in character. Yet the psalms never deviate from their primary purpose to be a book of prayer and praise, so that the teaching found therein is always expressive of or related to a personal experience and to an act of worship.

The Aspect of Blessing

There is in the Psalms a striking list of passages which when taken together describe the "blessed" or the "happy" man: the man whom we today would call "the God-fearing man."

They center around a plural Hebrew noun, *ashrey*, whose grammatical form always seems to call for some kind of a modifier. The first translation of the Old Testament, the Greek Septuagint, rendered it as an adjective, and it has continued in this form in most modern translations. Whether the primary meaning of the word is "blessedness" or "happiness" is a question for the exegesis of the commentator: opinions differ. The difference between the two is that "happy" suggests an inner and outward state of mind on the part of the worshipper, whereas "blessed" suggests something for which credit should be given to God as coming from him. My own opinion is that there is usually a little of each in the use of the word; although in at least one place, Psalm 137: 8-9, "blessed" seems definitely out of place. We shall see why later on in our study.

We have already met this unique word in the opening verses of Psalm 1. It occurs altogether 26 times in the Psalter. If we combine the 18 passages where RSV translates it as "blessed" (without ruling out the

133

concept of happiness) we get the following composite or ideal picture of a God-fearing man as experienced by the devout Israelite in life and in worship: "Blessed, or happy, is the man who fears and trusts in God; whose sins have been forgiven; whose place of refuge is in God and in his anointed; who delights to walk in the ways of God and to meditate on his Word, and who is faithful to his commandments; who considers the poor, and their needs, and keeps justice, and does righteousness, in everything; who is privileged to approach God in the fellowship of worship in his house; who finds his strength in the LORD, as he communes with him in prayer; who even when chastened is taught of God; who is one among a people whose God is Yahweh (the God of covenant revelation and redemption)." See Milton, *The Psalms*, 1954.

If as a good Bible student you are interested in knowing where to find the passages on which this composite picture is based we list them for you:

Psalm   1: 1-2 The man who delights in God's law.

Psalm   2: 12 All who take refuge in him.

Psalm   32: 1-2 The man who is forgiven, whose sin is covered.

Psalm   33: 12 The nation whose God is the Lord.

Psalm   34:   8 The man who takes refuge in him; that is, in the LORD. Here RSV has "happy" and ASV "blessed."

Psalm   40:   8 The man who makes the LORD his trust.

Psalm   41:   1 He who considers the poor.

Psalm   65:   4 He whom God chooses to dwell in his courts.

Psalm   84:   4 Those who dwell in God's house, singing praise.

Psalm   84:   5 The men whose strength is in God and whose heart is like a highway to Zion.

Psalm   84: 12 The man who trusts in the LORD of hosts.

Psalm   89: 15 The people who know the festal shout that accompanies true worship.

Psalm   94: 12 The man whom the LORD chastens and teaches.

Psalm 106:   3 They who observe justice and do righteousness.

Psalm 112:   1 The man who fears the LORD and delights in his commandments.

Psalm 119: 1-2 Those who walk in the way of the LORD blameless, who keep his testimonies, and who seek him wholeheartedly.

Psalm 128:   1 Every one who fears the LORD and walks in his ways.

While this tells us nothing about the way of salvation it is eloquent as to the way of life intended for God's people. It is still a legitimate part of our Hebrew-Christian heritage. It gives a faithful description of the God-fearing man, whether in the Old Testament or in the New. He is a man who is truly blessed or happy, because he fears God and loves his neighbor; and at the heart of his blessed life is the experience of forgiveness as the happiest of all human experiences.

The Aspect of Cursing

There is another group of psalms which create quite a problem for those who believe that the whole Bible is in some sense the Word of God, or who accept the Bible as the source of a genuine and credible Hebrew-Christian heritage. We call them sometimes the "imprecatory" psalms, and sometimes more simply the "curse" psalms. How shall we understand and use them as Christians who take both the Word of God and the love of God seriously?

Insofar as a psalm contains a prophetic denunciation of judgment against evil and the ways of evil men we have no real problem with them. They may indeed serve a good purpose in drawing a sharp distinction between good and evil, between right and wrong: a distinction which is too often blurred in the thoughts and actions of men today.

The same can perhaps be said about those psalms wherein the psalmist pleads for deliverance from enemies. Much depends upon the kind of language that he uses, for such a prayer is certainly not wrong in and of itself. To pray for rescue from the hand of our enemies is one thing; to pray for their destruction is something else.

The real problem arises when the declaration of judgment becomes *personal* instead of *prophetic*; or when there is evidence of a spirit of revenge, which on the face of it is contrary to the mind of Christ. As examples we would cite Psalm 69: 22-28, Psalm 109: 6-19, and Psalm 137: 8-9. I would suggest that you look them up and read them. We cannot get rid of them by ignoring their existence, as many Christian hymnals do when they include all of Psalm 137 except verses 8 and 9. We cannot account for them by saying that they belong to the Old Testament, for our Hebrew-Christian heritage draws from the Old Testament as well as the New. How shall we explain *the curse* in the devotional literature of the Old Testament?

The simplest explanation would be to say that the psalmists as sinful human beings sometimes spoke their own sinful thoughts rather than the thoughts of God. There is a significant sentence in the United Testimony on Faith and Life, which became the theological basis for the formation of the American Lutheran Church: "We reject all rationalizing processes which would explain away either the divine or the human factor in the Bible." Certainly we see the human factor vividly in the confession of sin. Might not sin be present where it is not confessed: where the sinner may indeed be altogether unaware of its presence. We might admit that this is not impossible; but what contribution would the curse psalms then make to our Hebrew-Christian heritage? If this were all that we could say about them, they would seem to be wholly the words and thoughts of sinful men, and in no sense whatever a revelation or word of God. As the New Testament says about the tongue as an untamed fire: "With it we bless the Lord and Father, and with it we curse men, who are made in the likeness of God. From the same mouth come blessing and cursing. My brethren, *this ought not to be so.*" (James 3: 9, 10). The apostle Paul says in Romans 12: 14, "Bless those who persecute you; bless and do not curse them." Even one of the curse psalms says much the same thing: "Let them curse, but do thou bless!" (Psalm 109: 28a). This is the same psalm which says of the wicked:

> "He loved to curse; let curses come on him!
>   He did not like blessing; may it be far from him!
> He clothed himself with cursing as his coat,
>   may it soak into his body like water,
>   like oil into his bones!" (Psalm 109: 17, 18)

What a strange inconsistency there seems to be here: where it is *right* for me to do what is *wrong* for others! If we leave the matter there we must expunge the curse psalms from our Hebrew-Christian heritage. The question is: must we leave the matter there?

Then the great C. S. Lewis in his *Reflections on the Psalms* would seem to possess a deeper insight. He does not deny the sinfulness of cursing, even in the Bible, nor does he attempt to defend the spirit of revenge. He simply insists that there must be some Christian use to be made even of these psalms: "that all Holy Scripture is in some sense — though not all parts of it in the same sense — the word of God." How so? It seems to me that he gives several good reasons for a Christian use of the curse psalms, in spite of their human frailty and sinfulness. The first is that in them I may see myself: they are like a mirror in which I may see "the same thing in my own heart"; and seeing myself as I am, and being made aware of the frequent desire for revenge that moves me to say things which I ought not to say because they cause others to be hurt, I experience in what I see *a revelation of God* that may hopefully lead me to repentance. The voice of God can reach me even through the sinfulness of a curse in which I recognize myself. The second reason probes more deeply into the human situation from which the cursing comes. As C. S. Lewis says, "It seemed to me that, seeing in them hatred undisguised, I saw also the natural result of injuring a human being." That is, *the guilt* for the curses uttered by someone else may be in me, or in the society of which I am a part. "I was the tempter." For cursing is a reaction to the sense of being wronged. It was so for the Jew who wrote Psalm 137, who felt deeply the injustice of the Babylonian Captivity and its attendant cruelties and lashed back in behalf of his people against the injustice. It may be so between individuals. The wrong experienced does not justify the curse, but it shifts some of the burden of responsibility for the curse on him who commits the wrong. In this sense the curse psalms may legitimately be used as a part of our Hebrew-Christian heritage. They may help to make us sensitive to the cruelty and injustice of our society, and perhaps of ourselves. The third reason mentioned by C. S. Lewis for the presence of the curse psalms in the Holy Scriptures is that they do help us to see more sharply the distinction between right and wrong. We shall not enlarge upon this point at any great length, but this sentence is worth quoting: "If the Jews cursed more bitterly than the Pagans this was, I think, at least in part because they took right and wrong more seriously." Whether from this source or from the Bible as a whole our Hebrew-Christian heritage certainly does take the distinction between right and wrong seriously. In this respect it would be well if our age could share its spirit.

There must be a limit to the length of this chapter as there is a limit to all things, and so we shall pause here: omitting other aspects of the Book of Psalms which have contributed their share to our Hebrew-Christian heritage. We would have no regrets in doing so if it were still true that the Book of Psalms were read with the same frequency that we as Christians read the New Testament. Is it still true?

Chapter 10

THE NEW TESTAMENT

It is surprising and significant how much of the teaching of the Old Testament is repeated and reaffirmed in the New. That is why we correctly speak of a Hebrew-Christian heritage, wherein the Jewish community and the Christian community share; but at the same time we have already noted some points at which the New Testament interpretation differs radically from that of Judaism. For example, the concept of the Fall and the doctrine of the sinful Nature of Man since the Fall are fundamental to New Testament theology, whereas in Jewish thought they are definitely minimized. What we want to do now is to point out the uniqueness of the New Testament and of the Christian interpretation, and in a sense to explain how two religions which have so much in common came to be so different. For make no mistake: there is a world of difference between present day Judaism and Christianity.

The Dominant Characteristic of Christianity

If we were to select one thing which makes the Christian religion unique it is the Person of Jesus Christ: his incarnation, his sinless life, his death on the Cross, his resurrection, his ascension, the hope of his coming again in glory.

It is difficult to illustrate this all-important point, for the illustration would include almost the whole of the New Testament. It is the uniqueness of Jesus Christ and of his claims upon us that makes the New Testament unique, and this uniqueness carries over into our Hebrew-Christian heritage so as to make it in a sense a Christian heritage. Yet, it is possible to be selective, and to illustrate something of the uniqueness in at least two different ways.

1. The first is to note some of the outstanding confessions of faith as to who he was and is.

There is the witness of John the Baptist as he said of Jesus beyond the river Jordan, "Behold, the Lamb of God, who takes away the sin of the world!" (John 1: 29). A little later he added, "And I have seen and borne witness that this is the Son of God." (John 1: 34). The Son of God and the Lamb of God: of no one, from Abraham and Moses to the greatest of the prophets, had this ever been said before. This confession belongs to the uniqueness of the Christian faith, and with it our Hebrew-Christian heritage is transformed into a uniquely Christian heritage.

Another witness to be noted is that of the angels at Bethlehem on the night of Jesus' birth: "for to you is born this day in the city of David a Savior, who is Christ the Lord" (Luke 2: 11). This is an assertion of the Messiahship and the Lordship and the Saviorhood of Jesus: each a breathtaking assertion which calls for careful consideration, and each a significant part of our Hebrew-Christian heritage as the New Testament interprets it.

Simon Peter said to Jesus, "You are the Christ, the Son of the living God" (Matthew 16: 16); and Jesus, instead of correcting an over-enthusiastic disciple, acknowledges the truth of his confession by saying, "Blessed are you, Simon Bar-Jona! For flesh and blood has not revealed this to you, but my Father who is in heaven" (Matthew 16:17). Here are two great assertions concerning Jesus: he is the Christ, or the Messiah; he is the Son of the living God.

The very name Jesus, which was given to him before his birth, is the Hellenized form of the Hebrew name Joshua, which means "Jehovah is salvation." It was a significant choice of name, which accurately describes what Jesus came to be, our Savior.

When Peter addressed the Jews on the Day of Pentecost he concluded his sermon about Jesus with these words: "Let all the house of Israel therefore know assuredly that God has made him both Lord and Christ, this Jesus whom you crucified" (Acts 2: 36). Again we have two significant assertions: Jesus is Lord; Jesus is the Christ, the Messiah.

According to John 1: 1, 14, "In the beginning was the Word, and the Word was with God, and the Word was God. — And the Word became flesh and dwelt among us, full of grace and truth; we have beheld his glory, glory as of the only Son from the Father." Again we have the confession of the unique Sonship of Jesus Christ.

In like manner the apostle Paul tells us in Philippians 2: 5-8 that though Jesus Christ "*was* in the form of God" he nevertheless took upon himself "the form of a servant," in order that he might become obedient unto death on a cross in our behalf. The sentences that follow in verses 9-11 deserve to be quoted in their entirety: "Therefore God has highly exalted him and bestowed on him the name which is above every name, that at the name of Jesus every knee should bow, in heaven and on earth and under the earth, and every tongue confess that Jesus Christ is Lord, to the glory of God the Father." In Colossians 1: 18 Paul puts it this way: "that in everything he might be preeminent." Jesus himself said, "I and the Father are one" (John 10: 30).

Do you begin to see what the New Testament means by *the uniqueness* of Jesus Christ? Of whom else has it been seriously said that he is the Messiah or the Christ, the Son of God, the Lamb of God, the Lord and Savior of all who believe, One with the Father in his preeminence and yet also one with humanity in his servanthood? It is *this claim* concerning Jesus Christ that makes the New Testament unique and which imparts a similar uniqueness to our Hebrew-Christian heritage at the point of its fulfillment in Christ.

2. There is another way whereby we can illustrate the uniqueness of Jesus Christ. It is by looking at some of the claims made by him and by his disciples concerning what he came to do.

We think of Jesus' words in Matthew 11: 27-30, "All things have been delivered to me by my Father; and no one knows the Son except the Father, and no one knows the Father except the Son and any one to whom the Son chooses to reveal him. Come to me, all who labor and are heavy-laden, and I will give you rest. Take my yoke upon you, and learn from me; for I am gentle and lowly in heart, and you will find rest for your souls. For my yoke is easy, and my burden is light."

We remember his words to Zacchaeus in Luke 19: 10, "For the Son of man came to seek and to save the lost."

We think of the words in "the little Bible," "For God so loved the world that he gave his only Son, that whoever believes in him should not perish but have eternal life. For God sent the Son into the world, not to condemn the world, but that the world might be saved through him." (John 3: 16-17).

We think of Peter's inspired words in Acts 4: 12, "And there is salvation in no one else, for there is no other name under heaven given among men by which we must be saved."

We think of the words of Paul in Romans 1: 16, 17: "For I am not ashamed of the gospel; it is the power of God for salvation to every one who has faith, to the Jew first and also to the Greek. For in it the righteousness of God is revealed through faith for faith; as it is written, 'He who through faith is righteous shall live.' "

Even more impressive are his words in Romans 8: 38-39, "For I am sure that neither death nor life, nor angels, nor principalities, nor things present, nor things to come, nor powers, nor height, nor depth, nor anything else in all creation, will be able to separate us from the love of God in Christ Jesus our Lord."

Or again, his words in Ephesians 1: 3-8, "Blessed be the God and Father of our Lord Jesus Christ, who has blessed us in Christ with every spiritual blessing in the heavenly places, even as he chose us in him before the foundation of the world, that we should be holy and blameless before him. He destined us in love to be his sons through Jesus Christ, according to the purpose of his will, to the praise of his glorious grace which he freely bestowed on us in the Beloved. In him we have redemption through his blood, the forgiveness of our trespasses, according to the riches of his grace which he lavished upon us."

We have already quoted extracts from Philippians 2: 5-11. Instead of further quotations let me suggest that the passage be read in its entirety. It leaves no doubt as to the uniqueness of Jesus Christ according to the faith of Paul.

The same is true of Colossians 1: 18-20, where we read: "He is the head of the body, the church; he is the beginning, the firstborn from the dead, that in everything he might be preeminent. For in him all the fullness of God was pleased to dwell, and through him to reconcile to himself all things, whether on earth or in heaven, making peace by the blood of his cross."

Paul's own personal confession of what he owed to Jesus Christ is found in I Timothy 1: 15-16: "The saying is sure and worthy of full acceptance, that Christ Jesus came into the world to save sinners. And I am the foremost of sinners; but I received mercy for this reason, that in me, as the foremost, Jesus Christ might display his perfect patience for an example to those who were to believe in him for eternal life."

To which we add this sentence concerning Christ from chapter 9: 12 of the Epistle to the Hebrews: "he entered once for all into the Holy Place, taking not the blood of goats and calves but his own blood, thus securing an eternal redemption."

And so we could continue indefinitely; for the united testimony of the New Testament is that Jesus Christ as the Son of God came into the world to redeem and to save sinners, and therefore that he came to save me. He is our Savior, and therefore also our Lord. If the Old Testament is theocentric or God-centered throughout, the New Testament is not only theocentric but also Christocentric or Christ-centered throughout. However much our Hebrew-Christian heritage has in common with Judaism, it is the uniqueness of Jesus Christ and of his work among men that transforms it ultimately into a Christian heritage: a heritage that centers in Jesus Christ as Lord and Savior.

The Element of Fulfillment in the New Testament

In his article on Old Testament Theology in *The Encyclopedia of the Lutheran Church (1965)*, H. W. Hertzberg stresses the fact that the two Testaments are bound together especially by the theme of "Promise-Fulfillment."

Actually the word "promise" may be too narrow in scope; for many of the "concepts" at which we have already looked in preceding chapters are *forward-looking* or *eschatological* in their implication, even if not worded in the form of a specific prophecy or promise.

For example: the doctrine of creation. We have quoted Edmond Jacob as saying that creation has *a beginning* and *a history* and *an end*, or *a goal*: that it is ultimately an *eschatological* concept. We speak often of the "creation chapters" at the beginning of Genesis; but we should be equally aware of the "creation chapters" at the end of the Book of Revelation. There will one day be "new heavens and a new earth in which righteousness dwells," as Peter also says in II Peter 3: 13. So also Paul, speaking of Man as a creature of God, says in II Corinthians 5: 17, "Therefore, if any one is in Christ, he is a new creation; the old has passed away, behold, the new has come." We would not understand our Hebrew-Christian heritage concerning creation if we did not recognize the New Testament "fulfillment" or consummation.

One of the clearest examples of the "Promise-Fulfillment" theme is the promise to Abraham, in Genesis 12: 1-3; with which is combined the covenant of blessing, "in you all the families of he earth will be blessed." We have seen already how this promise found a partial fulfillment in the history of Israel; and we have traced it to its spiritual fulfillment in Christ, as seen especially in Acts 3: 25-26, in Galatians 3, and in Ephesians 1: 3 ff. As F. N. Jasper has said, the fulfillment brings in "an element of novelty;" but the sequence from Abraham to Christ is abundantly clear.

The concept of Redemption, which in the Old Testament is associated primarily with the Exodus from Egypt and with the Return from the Babylonian Captivity, takes on a new dimension in the New Testament, where it is associated with the work of Christ. The redemption of Israel as a people from human bondage is a type of the redemption of the world from sin and death through the blood of Christ shed for us on the Cross. There is an element of "fulfillment" here; but again there is also an element of "novelty." The "fulfillment" is greater than the "prophecy" or the "promise" or the "symbol," whatever term we think most accurately describes the Old Testament "type" of things to come. Only on the basis of the Atonement of Jesus Christ can we confess with Christian assurance, "I believe that Jesus Christ, true God, begotten of the Father from eternity, and also true Man, born of the Virgin Mary, is my Lord; who has redeemed me, a lost and condemned creature, bought me and freed me from all sins, from death, and from the power of the devil; not with silver and gold, but with his holy and precious blood, and with his innocent sufferings and death; in order that I might be his own, live under him in his kingdom, and serve him in everlasting righteousness, innocence, and blessedness; even as he is risen from the dead, and lives and reigns to all eternity. This is most certainly true." (Martin Luther, Small Catechism). This is the very heart of "our Christian heritage:" or that which makes it unique and distinctive from "our Hebrew-Christian heritage," which it at the same time fulfills. At its center is the Person of Christ, of whom Paul writes in Ephesians 1: 7, 8, "In him we have redemption through his blood, the forgiveness of our trespasses, according to the riches of his grace which he lavished upon us." Hebrews 9: 12 puts it this way: "thus securing an eternal redemption."

Jesus speaks of still another "fulfillment" in the Sermon on the Mount: "Think not that I have come to abolish the law and the prophets; I have come not to abolish them, but to fulfill them." (Matthew 5: 17). There is a sense, of course, in which the Christian believer is *free from the law.* Any claims that it may have upon him as a Way of Salvation are null and void; for salvation is by grace alone through faith in the Lord Jesus Christ. But it might be questioned whether God ever intended the Law to be a Way of Salvation: was it not rather a Way of Life, in which God sought to guide his people *for their good always* (Deuteronomy 6: 24), a way which Samuel calls "the good and the right way" (I Samuel 12: 23) ? It is interesting that immediately after the words quoted above from Matthew 5: 17 Jesus launches into an exposition of several commandments from the Decalogue (the Moral Law), and after deepening our insight into their meaning and their proper application, he lets them stand with his signature underneath. So also in Matthew 22: 35-40, in answer to the question, "Teacher, which is the great commandment in the law?" he quotes Deuteronomy 6: 5 and Leviticus 19: 18 as a summary of the law and the prophets: giving the impression that it was his Teaching also. What the New Testament tries to tell us is to get things in their proper sequence: salvation by grace through faith first, then obedience to the will of God in every area of our life because we are children of God. The New Testament is full of admonitions and exhortations as to what is the will of God that the Christian disciple should believe and do. In fact, in the beginning Christianity was called simply "the Way": the only way by which we come to the Father, but also the way in which he would have us walk. In a book of daily devotions I read recently these significant words: "You who have come to Jesus, what was it you longed for when you came? You longed to have your sin forgiven and to find peace with God. But was your longing ended when you received this? No; you longed to get rid of sin from your heart and from your life. You *longed to become a good man.* You may not have expressed it that way, but this was what you longed for. And however poorly it has gone for you in your Christian life there is *still the indescribable longing to be a good man,* with the mind of Christ, and with a life directed by His Spirit." (Translation from the Swedish). This too is a part of our Hebrew-Christian heritage, which through Christ has been transformed into a Christian heritage.

But it is the Messianic Hope that constitutes the real essence of that "Promise-Fulfillment" motif which binds the two Testaments together. It cannot be otherwise if, as we have already said, it is the Person of Jesus Christ that makes the Christian religion unique. We can illustrate this "Messianic Hope" motif only briefly; it would require a reading of the whole New Testament to provide full proof of its uniquess. There is in the Old Testament the promise of *another prophet* like unto Moses (Deuteronomy 18: 15-22; cf. Acts 3: 22-23); the promise of *another king* like unto David (Isaiah 9: 1-7; Isaiah 11: 1-5; Micah 5: 2-4; Jeremiah 23: 5-6; Ezekiel 34: 23-24; cf. Matthew 22: 41-45); and the promise of a priest "after the order of Melchizedek" (Psalm 110: 4), who will also perform all those duties that are characteristic of every God-appointed priesthood (cf. Epistle to the Hebrews). *The Throne of David* by A. G. Hebert will help to give you a clear, full picture of this Messianic Hope which marks the New Testament fulfillment of the Old Testament. I have personally been helped to understand this Christological approach to the Old Testament prophecies by a pamphlet in German written by Ernst Sellin. The translated title is "The Old Testament in Christian Worship and Instruction." Like Hebert, the author says that we must understand this Christological approach in a broad sense, and not just in the narrow sense of direct verbal predictions (though the latter are not wholly excluded); and then he interprets what he means by this "broad sense" in these words: "It is impossible to separate the person of the Messiah as the Old Testament expected him from the rest of the Old Testament religion; in the first place, from the expectation of a coming of God himself, but in close connection with this, from the whole conception of God, of man, of sin, and of divine judgment and salvation." If you will think this statement through you will see that *practically everything* of which we have spoken in the first nine chapters of this book is *Messianically related*. A single passage from Isaiah 40: 10-11 will illustrate what Sellin means *by the coming of God himself* as being a part of the Messianic Hope:

"Behold, the Lord God comes with might,
    and his arm rules for him;
behold, his reward is with him,
    and his recompense before him.
He will feed his flock like a shepherd,
    he will gather the lambs in his arms,
he will carry them in his bosom,
    and gently lead those that are with young."

The New Testament counterpart is the passage concerning the good shepherd in John 10. In II Corinthians 5: 19 God's coming is expressed in this way: "God was in Christ reconciling the world to himself." Every other concept mentioned by Sellin could be illustrated with equal clarity.

Some Distinctive New Testament Teachings

If we were to select some of the more distinctive New Testament teachings which set the New Testament apart from the Old Testament, with which it has so much in common, I would list these four: 1) the concept of the kingdom of God; 2) the doctrine of the Holy Spirit; 3) the promise of eternal life as a free gift of God; and 4) a greater stress upon man's personal relationship, or his relationship as an individual, with God through faith in and obedience to the Lord Jesus Christ. Admittedly this list is limited in scope because of the limitations of space; but in itself it is not lacking in importance.

The Kingdom of God

We remember how prominent *the concept of the covenant* was in the Old Testament: the covenant with Abraham, the covenant renewed with Israel at Sinai, the covenant with the house of David, and the prophecy of a new covenant in Jeremiah 31: 31-34. Quite naturally this covenant concept carries over into the New Testament, where it finds its fulfillment in Christ and in his Church. But alongside of the covenant concept the New Testament puts even greater stress on the doctrine of the kingdom of God, or as it is sometimes called, the kingdom of heaven.

Both John the Baptist and Jesus the Christ began their preaching ministry with this keynote: "Repent, for the kingdom of heaven is at hand" (Matthew 3: 1, 2; Matthew 4: 17). There is no contradiction when Mark uses the words "The kingdom of God is at hand" (Mark 1: 15). Mark does, however, help us to see the coming of the kingdom in clearer perspective: "The time is fulfilled, and the kingdom of God is at hand; repent, and believe in the gospel." If I read this sentence aright it tells us three things: 1) the kingdom comes *as the fulfillment* of what God has said and done through his chosen people Israel: we might say that it is Messianically related; 2) the kingdom is *now present* in the person of the King, the Messiah, Jesus Christ; and 3) unlike any geographical or national kingdom *this kingdom is spiritual* in nature, and we enter it through the spiritual experiences of *repentance* and of *faith*: a repentance that leads to the forgiveness of sins, and faith that apprehends Jesus Christ as Lord and Savior. We recall that many of the parables of Jesus, for example in Matthew 13, deal with the kingdom of heaven. There is something to be learned from each parable; and yet, there are a few other passages that seem to me to be more important as illustrations of the uniqueness of the phrase in New Testament Teaching.

For example:

There are the words of Jesus to Peter in Matthew 16: 19, "I will give you the keys of the kingdom of heaven, and whatever you bind on earth shall be bound in heaven, and whatever you loose on earth shall be loosed in heaven." What Jesus is talking about here is a spiritual kingdom that reaches beyond earth into heaven: a kingdom based on the faith expressed in Simon Peter's confession, "You are the Christ, the Son of the living God."

Or consider the words of Jesus in Luke 12: 32. "Fear not, little flock, for it is your Father's good pleasure to give you the kingdom."

Or consider the words of Paul in Colossians 1: 13-14, "He has delivered us from the dominion of darkness and transferred us to the kingdom of his beloved Son, in whom we have redemption, the forgiveness of sins."

In Ephesians 5: 5 Paul rules out any *immoral* or *impure* or *covetous* man, whom he labels as an idolator, from "any inheritance in the kingdom of Christ and of God."

Or consider the words of Jesus in John 3: 5, "Truly, truly, I say to you, unless one is born of water and the Spirit, he cannot enter the kingdom of God."

My own two favorite passages are the *universal* reference to the kingdom in Revelation 11: 15, "The kingdom of the world has become the kingdom of our Lord and of his Christ, and he shall reign for ever and ever," and the *personal* reference in the words of the penitent thief on the Cross, "Jesus, remember me when you come in your kingly power" (Luke 23: 42; see footnote, "in your kingdom").

The interchange in translation between "kingdom" and "kingly power" is significant; for what is involved here *is* the kingly power of Jesus, or the recognition of him as the "King of kings," and the faith and hope to live under him in his kingdom both now and for ever. This is indeed a vital part of our Christian heritage.

The Doctrine of the Holy Spirit

Another significant aspect of the New Testament is its teaching concerning the Holy Spirit. The Old Testament also speaks of the Spirit of God, but not in the same personal sense as the New Testament does about the Holy Spirit. There is a uniqueness about the Day of Pentecost, and the outpouring of the Holy Spirit, which is comparable to the Incarnation of Christ. Read Acts 2 as the background for the full teaching of the New Testament concerning the Holy Spirit. It is a part of our Christian heritage that God who is One is also Triune: that is, we believe and confess the doctrine of Trinitarianism; we worship God the Father, God the Son, and God the Holy Spirit.

And yet, it is not with the doctrine that we are most concerned right now; of even greater importance is *the function* of the Holy Spirit. Jesus, in advance of Pentecost, referred to him as "the Spirit of truth," saying: "When the Spirit of truth comes, he will guide you into all the truth; for he will not speak on his own authority, but whatever he hears he will speak, and he will declare to you the things that are to come. He will

147

glorify me, for he will take what is mine and declare it to you. All that the Father has is mine; therefore I said that he will take what is mine and declare it to you." (John 16: 13-15). We note three significant things ascribed as functions of the Holy Spirit: to guide us into all truth, to declare the things to come, to glorify Jesus by representing him to us. Beginning here, we quickly discover that there are countless other verses with respect to the Holy Spirit's activity, of which we select but a few for quotation.

In Acts 1: 8 we read, "But you shall receive power when the Holy Spirit has come upon you; and you shall be my witnesses in Jerusalem and in all Judea and Sumaria and to the end of the earth." The Holy Spirit empowers us to witness for Christ as our Lord and our Savior.

In Romans 5: 5 we read, "and hope does not disappoint us, because God's love has been poured into our hearts through the Holy Spirit which has been given to us." The love of God *for us* in Christ Jesus our Lord is mediated *to us* by the Holy Spirit dwelling *within us*.

In Galatians 5: 22, 23, we have a most impressive list of the fruit of the Spirit in every Christian heart and life: "But the fruit of the Spirit is love, joy, peace, patience, kindness, goodness, faithfulness, gentleness, self-control; against such there is no law." It is the function of the Holy Spirit to enable us to do the will of God in every good thing. The fruit of the Spirit is in sharp contrast to the works of the flesh "which come naturally to us" as fallen, sinful creatures.

The refrain in Revelation 2-3, in the Letters to the Seven Churches, is a most significant admonition to every Christian: "He who has an ear, let him hear what the Spirit says to the churches." The New Testament abounds in admonitions by which the Holy Spirit seeks to guide and shape our life in the image of Christ. This is also the admonition of our Christian heritage to us: let us listen, let us hear, let us take heed to what the Holy Spirit says to us through the Word of God; and let us then together with the Spirit say "Come" to the Lord Jesus Christ who has promised to come again (Revelation 22: 17, 20).

The Promise of Eternal Life

The hope of resurrection, and the doctrine of the immortality of the soul, are not foreign to the Old Testament as some would have us believe; but it is only in the New Testament that we have a clear, direct promise of eternal life "through Jesus Christ our Lord."

The clearest of many statements to this effect is found in Romans 6: 23, "For the wages of sin is death, but the free gift of God is eternal life in Christ Jesus our Lord." We note especially two things in this statement: eternal life is a gift, a free gift of God, and it is inseparable from Jesus Christ. We receive it when we receive Jesus Christ as our living Lord and Savior. We may recall that Jesus not only called himself "the Way" and "the Truth" but also "the Life" (John 14: 6). The application as far as we are concerned is made by the apostle John, "And this is the testimony, that God gave us eternal life, and this life is in his Son. He who has the Son has life; he who has not the Son has not life." (I John 5: 11-12). Jesus himself defined eternal life in this way: "And this is eternal life, that they know thee the only true God, and Jesus Christ whom thou hast sent." (John 17: 3).

Eternal life is as simple, and as challenging, as these statements make it out to be. It is only by faith in Jesus Christ that eternal life becomes our priceless possession, here and now, and in heaven for ever. For mark the double emphasis in what we have just said. You simply have no right to try to separate the "other-worldly" from the "this-worldly" aspect of eternal life. That would be to deny the Risen, ever-living Christ, on whom we say that our faith and hope are built. Eternal life is an experience that begins *here and now* when we receive Jesus as our Savior. Eternal life is also an experience which *continues* beyond the grave if we die in faith in this living Savior. Despite what some theologians may say, the New Testament and our Christian heritage bear repeated witness to this promise of eternal life. It is among the most precious items of our heritage. Although the words do not occur in Romans 8: 38-39 the promise is there in those immemorable words of Paul, "For I am sure that *neither death, nor life,* nor angels, nor principalities, *nor things present, nor things to come,* nor powers, nor height, nor depth, *nor anything else in all creation,* will be able to separate us from the love of God in Christ Jesus our Lord." This is the assurance that only the promise of eternal life can give; and it is a part of our Christian heritage.

There are frequent variations on the same theme. Not without reason does the New Testament speak of "eternal salvation" (Hebrews 5: 9) and "eternal redemption" (Hebrews 9: 12) and "the promised eternal inheritance" (Hebrews 9: 15) and "eternal glory" (I Peter 5: 10) and "the eternal kingdom of our Lord and Savior Jesus Christ" (II Peter 1: 11) in helping us to see just a little of the glorious "other-worldliness" of the promise of "eternal life." This does not rule out the equally glorious

149

fact that we can begin to experience eternal life *when we receive Jesus Christ,* who is the life, and the giver of life. If we have him we have life, now and eternally. Such is our Christian heritage.

The Personal Nature of the Christian Religion

There are a great many other New Testament teachings worthy of consideration and distinctive of our Christian heritage; but we shall conclude by noting the intensely personal character of religion as set forth in the New Testament: that is, of the Christian religion.

In a sense this brings us back to the beginning of the chapter, where we noted that the one unique factor in the Christian religion and therefore in our Christian heritage is the Person of Jesus Christ. What we would stress now is the personal relationship of each believer to this Christ.

In the Old Testament the religious emphasis is more on the community, the people of Israel, and also largely on life in this world. We do not mean to exaggerate. There is personal religion also in the Old Testament, especially in the Psalms; and there is certainly some awareness of what we call "other-worldliness." In the New Testament, however, the personal emphasis is to the fore: not to the exclusion of the community in the form of the Church, but certainly with constant awareness of the relationship between each redeemed, repentant, forgiven sinner and the Savior, the Lord Jesus Christ. Faith, hope, and love, the Pauline trinity of things which abide, are personal in nature or they are nothing. John 3: 16, sometimes called "the little Bible," begins on a note of *universalism* but concludes on a note of *particularism*: "For God so loved the world that he gave his only Son, that whoever believes in him should not perish but have eternal life." And so it is throughout the New Testament. The question that confronts us everywhere is this: What do you think of Jesus Christ? What will you do with him, in your heart, in your life? Will you trust him as your Savior and serve him as your Lord?

The question of your relation to Jesus Christ as Lord and Savior permits no evasion. What you do thereafter as a member of his Church and as a citizen in the community is significant, but the relationship witih God through faith in Jesus Christ is all-important: and it is strictly personal, between you and your God. Such has been the clear witness of our Christian heritage down through the ages, and nothing or no one can make it otherwise today. As Paul says in Galatians 2: 20, "I have been crucified with Christ; it is no longer I who live, but Christ who lives in me; and the life I now live in the flesh I live by faith in the Son of God, who loved me and gave himself for me." Equally personal is his confession in Philippians 1: 21, "For to me to live is Christ, and to die is gain."

We close with the words of Jesus in John 6: 35-37, "I am the bread of life; he who comes to me shall not hunger, and he who believes in me shall never thirst. But I said to you that you have seen me and yet do not believe. All that the Father gives me will come to me; and him who comes to me I will not cast out."

You cannot make Christianity more personal than that! This is our Christian heritage. Thank God that each one of us may share in it if we will: that it belongs to our inheritance as children of God.

CONCLUSION

In the Foreword we raised two questions as to the theme of Our Hebrew-Christian Heritage: we said that such a theme should stimulate *curiosity* as to what it means and also *concern* as to its continuing relevance today.

We have tried thus far *to satisfy the curiosity* as to the meaning or the content of Our Hebrew-Christian Heritage. For anyone who is willing to use these ten chapters as a study-guide *the essentials of that heritage* should become quite clear. The chapter headings provide a fairly adequate outline of what we have tried to cover: the concepts of God, of Creation, of Man (including the Fall), of Election, Covenant, and Mission, of Redemption, of Torah (in the sense of Teaching as well as of Law), of Prophecy, of History, of Psalmody, and of the New Testament (with its uniqueness centering in the Person of Jesus Christ as Lord and Savior and Son of God). In each chapter, however, we found it necessary to select a few of the most significant aspects and illustrations of the main theme; for it is impossible to give what we might call "complete coverage" to any doctrine without looking at the Holy Scriptures as a whole. That is to say, our Hebrew-Christian Heritage is too rich in substance or content to permit a condensation that does not omit some very essential things. Nevertheless I dare to hope that in these chapters we have brought to life something of the throbbing essence of that religious heritage which has belonged to the Christian Church from the days of its beginning, including that which it shared with early Judaism as well as that which made it uniquely Christian; and that some who read these chapters with care will thank God for so rich a heritage, and that it is our heritage still today.

For the ultimate question is just this: is Our Hebrew-Christian Heritage still valid in this 20th century A.D., or is it now out-of-date? It is a sad fact that we live in a day and age when the Judaeo-Christian tradition is rejected and scorned by many, and that in the place of our Hebrew-Christian Heritage a new and different religion is substituted. The earmark of this "new religion" is "humanism," when man's religious concern does not begin with "the living God" and with the Lord Jesus Christ as the one and only Savior from sin, death, and the power of the devil, but rather with the problem of human relations. We shall not delve at length into this "new religion," because for our purpose it is not necessary to do so. The question that inevitably thrusts itself upon us is this: can we as 20th century citizens, who also want to be known as Christian, still receive and rejoice in our Heritage as we have studied it, and can we still pass it on in faith as a worthwhile bequest to coming generations?

My own answer to that question is clear from what I have already written. It is an emphatic Yes. The problem arises, however, when we try to heed the admonition of Peter in I Peter 3:15, "Always be prepared to make a defense to any one who calls you to account for the hope that is in you, yet do it with gentleness and reverence." We frankly admit that we accept our Heritage on the basis of faith rather than proof. For instance, I am firmly convinced that *there is a living God,* but I cannot prove it to you or to any one else: I can only confess it as an experience of faith. And so it is all down the line of the doctrines that belong to Our Hebrew-Christian Heritage.

But if I cannot prove what I believe, neither can you or any one else disprove what I believe. It can be rejected as a Christian Heritage; but it has not been, or can ever be, disproved at any vital point. And it is a Heritage which satisfies my faith! It is a Heritage which still challenges us to try it out in faith, and in so doing to experience the truth of it. Let me repeat: Our Hebrew-Christian Heritage has not been and never can be disproved. It can be disregarded; it can be denied; it can be disapproved by those who do not like it but instead prefer some sort of a substitute: but we repeat again, it never has been and never can be disproved. It moves in a different world than that of science, the world of faith. We grant that this is a negative way of approaching the issue of its continued relevance; but it is nevertheless an adequate reply to those who would cast this Hebrew-Christian Heritage aside as of no value, without so much as giving it an honest trial. What the Christian Church needs today is a host of witnesses who have been willing to try it in faith and have found that it works: it satisfies; it lives up to its promises; it is a Heritage to be joyfully received and then to be just as joyfully passed on. It is only when our Christian Heritage has not been honestly tried that it has seemed to be a disappointment. The plea of this little book is that our generation too be willing to accept their Heritage and to discover what a joy it can be! And then to pass it on, so that we do not disinherit God's people who come after us!

BIBLIOGRAPHICAL INDEX
Numbers at end of each entry indicate page numbers
where the work is quoted in this book.

Alleman, Herbert C., and Flack, Elmer E., *O. T. Commentary* 1948 — 28, 57.

Augustana Explanation to *Luther's Catechism,* 1939 — 28, 75.

Barton, G. A., *Archeology and the Bible* — 23.

Bonhoeffer, Dietrich, *Creation and Fall,* Macmillan, 1965 — 21, 28.

Book of Concord, Tappert's edition, 1959 — 28.

Buttrick, George A., *Christ and Man's Dilemma* — 40, 46.

Davidson, A. B., *The Theology of the Old Testament,* 1904 — 77.

Delitzsch, Franz, *Commentary on the Psalms,* Eng. tr. 1871 — 129.
Messianic Prophecies, 1890 Eng. tr. 1891 — 104.

Fritsch, Charles T., *The Layman's Bible Commentary* — 56.

Girdlestone, R. F., *Synonyms of the Old Testament,* reprint 1948 — 12.

Hebert, A. G., *The Throne of David,* 1941 — 91, 94, 144.

Hertz, J. H., *The Pentateuch and Haftorahs* — 43.

Hertzberg, Hans Wilhelm, *The Encyclopedia of the Lutheran Church,* 1965 — 14, 142.
Commentary on the Book of Samuel — 116.

Jacob, Edmond, *Theology of the Old Testament,* 1958 — 10, 15, 22, 47, 48, 49.
A Companion to the Bible (article; "Man") — 32, 42, 49.

Kevan, E. F., "Genesis", *The New Bible Commentary* 1953 — 28.

Keyser, Leander S., *Man's First Disobedience* — 40.

Lewis, C. S., *Reflections on the Psalms* — 136.

Lutheran Service Book and Hymnal, 1958 — 20.

Marshall, Robert, *The Mighty Acts of God* — 11, 90.

McCaul, *Aids to Faith* — 12.

McFadyen, J. E., *A Cry for Justice,* 1912 — 96.

Milton, John, *God's Covenant of Blessing,* Straus, 1965 — 48, 54, 57, 68, 94.
Prophecy Interpreted — 91.
The Bible: Book of Faith, Augsburg, 1964 — 21.
The Psalms, 1954 — 134.

Moffatt, James, *The Bible, A New Translation,* 1950 — 115.

Moller, Wilhelm, *Inledning till Gamla Testamentet,* tr. from German, 1935 — 55.

Nillson, Kjell-Ove, *Genom tron allena,* an anthology of Luther's sermons, 1967 — 31.

Paterson, John, *The Goodly Fellowship of the Prophets,* 1953 — 89, 90, 91.

Pieters, Albertus, *Notes on Genesis* — 27.

Proksch, Otto, *Theology of the Old Testament* (German edition) — 54.

Richardson, Alan, A Theological Word *Book of the Bible* — 76, 90. *Commentary on Genesis I-XI,* 1953 — 33.

Ridderbos, N. H., *Is There a Conflict Between Genesis I and Natural Science?* — 26, 29.

Ringgren, Helmer, *Faith of the Psalmists* — 117.

Rowley, H. H., *The Faith of Israel* — 10.

Thieliche, Helmut, *How the World Began* — 22, 27, 32, 35.

Tresmontant, Claude, *A Study of Hebrew Thought* — 22, 50, 90, 91, 111, 115.

Turton, W. H., *The Truth of Christianity,* 1925 —6.

Vawter, Bruce, *Paths Through Genesis* — 57.

von Rad, Gerhard, *Commentary on Genesis* — 25, 26, 27, 29, 44, 46, 50, 56, 62. *Moses* — 17, 20, 127.

Wahlstrom, Eric, *God Who Redeems* — 61.

Westerman, Claus, *A Thousand Years and A Day,* 1962 — 28, 34.

Westminster Dictionary of the Bible, 1944 — 25, 76, 80, 89, 90, 92, 116.

Wevers, John Wm., *The Way of Righteousness* — 117.

Wingren, Gustav, *An Exodus Theology* — 62, 71. *Creation and the Law* — 21, 75.

Wright, G. Ernest, *The Challenge of Israel's Faith,* 1944 — 10, 14.

Wright, G. Ernest, and Fuller, Reginald H., *The Book of the Acts of God,* 1957 — 11, 59, 109, 116, 117.